PRAISE FO
AND MAND

"A joyful book filled with highly achievable food. Simply Malaysian is simply brilliant and I can't wait to get cooking from it." MEERA SODHA

"My stomach started rumbling when I flicked through Simply Malaysian. The combination of flavours instantly connects me to my dad's Malaysian heritage, bringing back memories of family feasts and hawker-stall favourites. What makes this cookbook truly special is how Mandy transforms these beloved dishes into approachable recipes using ingredients I can actually find at my local grocery store. This is a cookbook for anyone who wants a little taste of Malaysia in their kitchen." RACHEL KHOO

"Mandy's recipes are easy, delicious and full of flavour. A must have book." CHING HE HUANG

"Mandy's food is real, wonderful, exciting, classic and contemporary all at the same time. To know and understand the secrets of great Malaysian food, as cooked and orchestrated by Mandy, would be a revelation for anyone, from budding amateur to the most experienced cook." JOHN TORODE

To Rhion, I have written this book so
that you will be able to cook like I have
for you when I am no longer with you.
With all my love.

SIMPLY MALAYSIAN

EVERYDAY DISHES
TO COOK AT HOME

MANDY YIN

Photography by Louise Hagger

Quadrille

CONTENTS

INTRODUCTION

Simply Malaysian features over 80 accessible, quick and affordable Malaysian-inspired recipes for the home cook.

Within two weeks of publishing *Sambal Shiok* (my first baby), my son, Rhion, was born. It was such a busy time and between promoting the book and juggling life as a parent and running a restaurant, there were many challenges along the way, some of which nearly pushed me towards breaking point. These experiences encouraged me to write this book, as I hope it may help to inspire your mealtimes and make your life easier.

Nowadays, I have less time to make the project-style recipes that my first book showcased, but cooking fabulous food at home still brings me much joy. At home I have adopted a more pared-back approach to cooking. This book encapsulates how I cook daily in my home kitchen, with as few ingredients, as little preparation, mess and washing up, and as quickly as possible. I rely heavily on store-bought sauces widely available in Western supermarkets or online, but my home-cooking is bolstered by a few pantry staples that I make myself.

My priority these days is fast, simple, no-stress food to feed my small family as efficiently and effectively as possible. This book shows that it is still possible to eat incredible Malaysian-inspired food at home daily. These recipes also happen to be very affordable, as it is normal to add vegetables to bulk up Malaysian dishes, using long braises as well as finely slicing and velveting proteins with cornflour (cornstarch) to make cheaper cuts go further. Day-to-day, Malaysians will always prioritize affordability when cooking at home.

Malaysian home-cooked dinners usually include one meat dish, one vegetable-focused dish and, if the cook is feeling up to it, maybe an egg dish or a soup. Accompanied, of course, by plenty of rice to mop up the various sauces.

'Economy rice' eateries are also extremely popular in Malaysia, where you are handed a plate of steamed white rice before you proceed to help yourself to however much you like from a choice of 20 to 50 different dishes. Malaysian Chinese also frequently go out to eat at dai chow/zi char restaurants – casual, family-run eateries that serve a wide variety of home-style Chinese dishes. If you have visited economy rice or dai chow eateries, you'll get an idea of what Malaysians cook at home.

Xigong Seafood Restaurant, Kuala Lumpur © Guan Chua

Hoong Yuen, Kuala Lumpur © Guan Chua

Lubuk Bangku, Kuala Lumpur © Guan Chua

Restoran Suri Masakan Melayu Asli, Perlis © Guan Chua

All of the recipes are easy, quick, affordable and incredibly tasty. The book starts off with my store-cupboard staples. A stonking chapter on rice, noodles and pasta follows, which includes several one-pot wonders. Next come the ingredient-led chapters (split into vegetables and pulses, eggs, meat and poultry, fish and seafood) wherein the dishes are designed to accompany plenty of rice. Maximum impact, minimum fuss. Recipes meant for you to come back to, again and again!

If you are willing to stir-fry, make a roast or whip up a curry or stew, then this book will be right up your street. Perfect for the beginner cook, a gift for your child leaving home for university, a busy working millennial or Gen Z, or someone like myself – a sleep- and time-deprived first-time parent!

My son Rhion eating soy-braised chicken from page 140

INGREDIENTS

All of the recipes in this book focus on using Asian ingredients and store-bought sauces now widely available in Western supermarkets and commonly found in the Western pantry; in particular chillies, coconut milk, dried spices, curry powder, soy sauce, sesame oil, fish sauce, oyster sauce, rice vinegar and Thai red curry paste.

I have included just a handful of ingredients that you can order online or pick up from your local East Asian supermarket, such as shrimp paste, yellow bean sauce, dried shrimp and dried Chinese mushrooms. A little goes a long way with these more unusual but umami-laden ingredients, as small amounts will pack a big punch of flavour. Once you have these in your arsenal, a massive range of exciting new dishes will enter your repertoire.

Ketchup and tamarind also feature heavily in this book. Malaysians are very fond of ketchup due to our British colonial past. Tamarind grows easily in Malaysia and is prized for its sourness. The Malay word *assam* means 'sour' or 'tamarind' interchangeably. If you don't have tamarind paste, Worcestershire sauce (I use Lea & Perrins) is a wonderful substitute and sometimes actually adds more to a dish than using tamarind would!

If you find that you are missing one or two basic store-bought sauces, please don't worry. These recipes are very forgiving and you can just taste at the end of cooking and add a touch more salt/sugar/pepper/chilli sauce/chilli oil to your liking, to make up for whatever it is you're missing.

As a side note, I have in the past tried to get on board with store-bought garlic or ginger pastes, but have decided that these are just not suited to my cooking because they tend to include salt and water. I don't like garlic or ginger sputtering at me if I'm trying to stir-fry. Store-bought minced/chopped garlic or ginger are preserved in vinegar, which I find taints the flavour. So I much prefer to peel a few bulbs of garlic every fortnight or so and finely chop in a food processor before storing in a clean jar, so that I have fresh garlic ready to go. I also prefer to use ginger as fresh as possible.

I like to buy large bunches of coriander (cilantro) and will always have some spring onions (scallions) knocking about, both ready to bring an extra element of freshness and a layer of flavour to whatever I'm serving.

At the start of this book you will find four recipes for larder must-haves. I have tried to make use of store-bought sauces and condiments as much as possible, but spending a bit of time making these four workhorses every so often will help keep some stellar dishes in your weekly meal planning.

COOKING NOTE

I have tried to write this book so that you have all the information in terms of ingredient prompts, substitutes, utensils and equipment within each recipe. The only additional piece of information is that I have gas hobs (stove burners) at home, with a range of small, medium and large rings. The recipes will also work fine with induction hobs. I always start off cooking using the largest hob appropriate for the wok or pan required for the recipe, and where the recipe says to 'reduce the heat to the lowest possible level', I will move the wok or pan onto the smallest hob.

SHOPPING LIST

These are my preferred brands of various store-cupboard ingredients used throughout this book, as well as general notes which might be helpful to you.

CHILLI OIL
Sun Wah Chilli Oil with Shrimp and **Tean's Gourmet Sambal Ranggup Ikan Bilis Halus Crispy Anchovy Chilli** are both truly delicious and their flavour profiles complement Malaysian cooking. Otherwise **Lao Gan Ma**'s ubiquitous crispy chilli in oil is widely available.

CHILLI SAUCE
Maggi Malaysian Chilli Sauce with Garlic. If you can't be bothered to make my Tomato Sambal on page 28, I prefer this Maggi chilli sauce to Sriracha, but if you can't get it, then Sriracha will do!

COCONUT MILK AND COCONUT CREAM
Chaokoh, Aroy D and **Kraw Thip** coconut milk for their high coconut milk content and lack of emulsifiers.

I don't have a preference for any brand of UHT cartons/cans of coconut cream. The different brands I have tried to date are very similar in composition. Just be sure not to use the dense blocks of coconut cream for the recipes in this book as they require the more liquidy UHT version to give a lovely viscous sauce.

CURRY POWDER
Adabi Meat Curry Powder. Try to source a Malaysian curry powder online as it'll give you an incredible depth of flavour, even if it isn't Adabi.

DRIED SHRIMP
Jeeny's Premium Quality Dried Shrimp. You can find these online or in the chiller or freezer sections of East Asian supermarkets.

DRIED CHINESE MUSHROOMS
I don't have a preference for these. Just be aware that these come in different sizes, the larger ones typically being more expensive. This is why I have given the weight whenever these dried mushrooms are used in the recipes so that you use the correct amount no matter what size you have in your pantry.

DRY SPICES
Rajah brand for all dry spices – ground turmeric, ground coriander, ground cumin, fennel seeds, chilli powder, fine/coarse ground black pepper, garlic powder, ground ginger, ground white pepper, green cardamom and cloves.

FISH SAUCE
I like **Squid** brand and it is widely available.

KETCHUP
Heinz tomato ketchup is unrivalled.

MAKRUT (KAFFIR) LIME LEAVES
You can find these fresh in some large Western supermarkets, or buy them frozen online. Avoid dried lime leaves as these have a very muted flavour.

OYSTER SAUCE
For oyster sauce, you must seek out the premium version as the cheaper ones have very little oyster content and are much too salty. Simply buy anything that says '**Premium Oyster Sauce**' on the label. If you are vegetarian, vegetarian stir-fry sauce with mushroom is a good substitute. Gluten-free oyster sauce is also now widely available.

RICE VINEGAR
Amoy white rice vinegar has the perfect balance of acidity with a hint of sweetness.

RED CURRY PASTE

Thai Mae Ploy Red Curry Paste. I like this as it doesn't contain artificial MSG, colourings or preservatives. It also has a great fragrance from lime leaves, galangal and high-quality shrimp paste. This brand is also not too salty.

(SHAOXING) RICE WINE

Taijade Shaohsing Rice Wine is my go to. You can use Harvey's Bristol Cream sherry as a substitute.

SAMBAL TUMIS

If you don't have time to make my Sambal Tumis cooked chilli sauce on page 29, then **Woh Hup Sambal Ikan Bilis Paste** is a fantastic store-bought version full of flavour from dried anchovies.

SESAME OIL

Both **Amoy** and **Yeo's pure sesame oils** have a glorious nutty flavour and a lovely smoky fragrance. Otherwise just make sure to use bottles which are clearly labelled 'pure' sesame oil, as blended sesame oils simply aren't the real deal.

SHRIMP PASTE

Thai Nang Fah (Tue Kung) Shrimp Paste is easier to handle than Malaysian/Indonesian blocks of *belacan* as it is soft enough to be scooped out with a spoon. None of the dishes in this book require shrimp paste to be dry-toasted before using, and so the softer scoopable Thai version is perfect.

SOY SAUCES

Kikkoman Light Soy Sauce. My mum has always used this and I love the little (refillable) pouring bottle. I find it isn't overly salty and has a lovely rounded finish to it. I also like **Amoy Gold Label Light Soy Sauce** as it has a similar flavour profile. If you are gluten intolerant, use any gluten-free light soy sauce.

Pearl River Bridge Superior Dark Soy Sauce. Dark soy sauce is used to add a darker, more attractive caramel colour to some dishes, particularly sauces that use cornflour (cornstarch) as a thickening agent, or stir-fried noodles to accentuate the *wok hei* (breath of the wok). It is less salty than light soy sauce. If you are gluten intolerant, use any gluten-free dark soy sauce.

Habhal's Sweet Soya Bean Sauce. This kecap manis sweet soy sauce is made in Johor, Malaysia, so it will give you a great result for these recipes.

TAMARIND PASTE

Namjai Pure Tamarind Paste is the thickest and most concentrated I have found; otherwise look for versions with at least 50% tamarind content. If using other more watery brands, you may need to increase how much you use. If you cannot find tamarind paste at all, Lea & Perrins Worcestershire sauce is an excellent substitute and sometimes works even better than tamarind because of the added umami from anchovy!

YELLOW BEAN SAUCE

I like **Amoy Salted Yellow Bean Sauce** or **Amoy Crushed Yellow Bean Sauce** as neither contains any artificial MSG. The salted yellow bean tends to be slightly more umami with bits of yellow bean still apparent for more texture, whereas the crushed yellow bean sauce is smoother and a tad sweeter. Either will work for the recipes in this book that call for yellow bean sauce. If you can't find yellow bean sauce or are gluten intolerant, use white shiro miso paste as a substitute.

MENU SUGGESTIONS

MELLOW PROTEINS WITH SPICY VEG

Savoury egg custard with soy and sesame
(page 119)

Omelette with onions, chillies and soy
(page 126)

Corned beef egg hash
(page 122)

Lime, coriander and shrimp paste chicken
(page 139)

Soy braised chicken
(page 140)

Sesame ginger chicken
(page 146)

Braised pork belly with ginger, vinegar and soy
(page 154)

Nyonya tamarind pork belly
(page 160)

Soy and garlic lamb chops
(page 135)

Cod with fish sauce, chillies, ginger and basil
(page 187)

Greg's sweet and sour fish
(page 193)

Trout with tamarind, Chinese mushrooms
and celery (page 199)

Prawns with spring onions, ginger and tomato
(page 202)

+

Spring greens and chickpea curry
(page 85)

Green Turkish peppers with anchovies
(page 96)

Sambal aubergines and okra
(page 79)

Sambal tenderstem broccoli
(page 100)

Aubergines in spicy yellow bean sauce
(page 106)

Yellow vegetable curry
(page 99)

On pages 16, 17 and 18, pick and choose dishes from the left-hand side column to go with dishes on the right-hand side. For two people, aim to serve two dishes in total, along with plenty of rice. This will probably result in leftovers that can be frozen, or for another meal later on in the week. For four people, I would still serve two dishes along with rice – there wouldn't be leftovers in this case. If you're entertaining, I would serve the same number of dishes as there are diners, to go with rice, for a more lavish meal. The vast majority of the recipes in this book can be made in advance and reheated when your guests arrive.

SPICY PROTEINS WITH MELLOW VEG

Fried eggs with bird's eye chillies and soy
(page 112)

Spiced baked egg custard with fish
(page 129)

Golden fragrant chicken
(page 145)

Hannah's lazy chilli chicken
(page 148)

Feng pork belly
(page 159)

Lamb and potato curry
(page 163)

Black beef stew
(page 170)

Beef curry with dried shrimp
(page 175)

Sambal skate wing
(page 182)

Salmon with ginger, honey and chilli
(page 188)

Haddock with yellow bean and chilli oil
(page 194)

Hot sour tamarind fish curry (page 196)

Spicy tomato prawns (page 201)

Greg's spicy fried prawns (page 183)

+

Watercress and anchovy soup (page 74)

Creamed spinach with dried shrimp
(page 80)

Green beans and soy
(page 82)

Shrimp paste fried cabbage
(page 86)

Chayote with dried shrimp and glass noodles
(page 88)

Creamy Savoy cabbage and celery
(page 93)

Ginger spring onion beansprouts
(page 103)

Okra with mustard seeds
(page 104)

Charred Chinese leaves with fish sauce
(page 109)

NICE TEXTURAL COMBINATIONS

Soft and dry carb

Chicken, bacon and mushroom rice (page 35)

One-pot chicken rice (page 45)

Spam egg fried rice (page 59)

Beef and tomato rice (page 66)

+ Crunchy veg

Green beans and soy (page 82)

Shrimp paste fried cabbage (page 86)

Creamy Savoy cabbage and celery (93)

Charred Chinese leaves with fish sauce (page 109)

Soupy protein

Pork rib and daikon soup (page 153)

ABC soup with macaroni (page 62)

+ Spicy crunchy veg

Green Turkish peppers with anchovies (page 96)

Okra and mustard seeds (page 104)

Dry protein

Corned beef egg hash (page 122)

Hainanese roast chicken (page 134)

Lime, coriander and shrimp paste chicken (139)

Maxine's turmeric roast chicken (page 151)

Spicy coconut roast chicken (page 142)

+ Saucy veg

Watercress and anchovy soup (page 74)

Chayote with dried shrimp and glass noodles (page 88)

Creamed spinach with dried shrimp (page 80)

Yellow vegetable curry (page 99)

Ginger spring onion beansprouts (page 103)

JUST ADD RICE FOR A FULLY-BALANCED MEAL

Scrambled eggs with chayote (page 125)

Tomato eggs with oyster sauce (page 117)

Spring greens and chickpea curry (page 85)

Omelette with fine beans and oyster sauce
(page 114)

Stir-fried minced pork with green beans
(page 156)

Lamb mince curry (page 166)

Lamb curry with coriander and spinach
(page 169)

Black pepper beef (page 172)

Hainanese beef stew (page 176)

Tom yum mussels (page 204)

ALTERNATIVE ROASTS / SUMMER BARBECUES

Hainanese roast chicken (page 134)

Lime, coriander and shrimp paste chicken
(page 139)

Spicy coconut roast chicken (page 142)

Maxine's turmeric roast chicken (page 151)

Soy and garlic lamb chops (page 135)

Sambal skate wing (page 182)

Haddock with yellow bean and chilli oil
(page 194)

VEGETARIAN ONE-POT MEALS

DIY Indomie (page 51)

Green pasta with chilli and cumin (page 60)

Spring greens and chickpea curry (page 85)

Malaysian mushroom and bean stew (page 75)

Spiced baked beans (page 94)

Omelette with fine beans and oyster sauce (page 114)

VEGETARIAN PAIRINGS WITH RICE

Silken tofu with fried shallots, sesame and soy (page 91)	+	Green beans and soy (page 82)
Omelette with onions, chillies and soy (page 126)	+	Ginger spring onion beansprouts (page 103)
Scrambled eggs with chayote (page 125)	+	Aubergines in spicy yellow bean sauce (page 106)
Yellow vegetable curry (page 99)	+	Fried eggs with bird's eye chillies and soy (page 112)
Sambal aubergines and okra (page 79)	+	Savoury egg custard with soy and sesame (page 119)

HOMEMADE MUST-HAVES

SHALLOT OIL

Makes 200g (7oz)

A little shallot oil adds such magic to so many dishes. I always make quite a large batch, as it keeps well in an airtight glass jar in a cool, dry place for months.

200ml (scant 1 cup) vegetable oil
100g (3½oz) banana or round
Asian shallots (peeled weight),
finely sliced

Heat the oil in a small saucepan over a medium heat for around 5 minutes. The oil is hot enough when a quick, steady stream of bubbles rise around a single wooden chopstick held upright in the oil.

Fry the shallots, stirring every 30 seconds or so, as those around the sides of the pan will cook quicker. The shallots will continue cooking in the residual heat, so be sure to remove them from the oil as soon as they have turned light golden brown. This should take around 3½ minutes.

Take the saucepan off the heat. Use a small, fine-mesh sieve to drain the shallots from the oil and spread them evenly across a clean plate lined with a paper towel to stop them cooking too much more. Leave the shallots and oil to cool.

When the shallots and oil have cooled, combine them in a sterilized glass jar to store.

The following recipes use this shallot oil:

DIY Indomie (page 51)

Congee with Chicken and Ginger (page 54)

Beef and Tomato Rice (page 66)

Silken Tofu with Fried Shallots, Sesame and Soy (page 91)

Savoury Egg Custard with Soy and Sesame (page 119)

GINGER SPRING ONION SAUCE

Makes 220g (7¾oz)

This deceptively simple sauce is the secret to recreating many Cantonese dishes. It is incredibly useful as the base of a stir-fry or as a dipping sauce. If you don't have a food processor, you can just finely slice the spring onions (scallions) and finely chop the ginger by hand. It keeps refrigerated for months.

5cm (2in) ginger (50g/1¾oz starting weight), peeled and finely chopped
80g (2¾oz) spring onions (scallions), cut into 2.5cm (1in) pieces
¾ tsp table salt
2 tsp white rice vinegar
110ml (scant ½ cup) vegetable oil

Use a small food processor to finely chop the ginger, then transfer the chopped ginger to a medium saucepan.

Add the spring onions to the same food processor bowl and use the pulse function to roughly chop them. Make sure not to press the food processor button down continuously, otherwise you will end up with spring onion purée, which is not what you want for this recipe.

Transfer the spring onions to the saucepan and add the salt and vinegar. Stir to combine and spread out over the bottom of the pan.

Warm the oil in a separate small saucepan over a high heat until a steady stream of bubbles rises from a single wooden chopstick held upright in the oil. The oil should take around 5 minutes to reach the right temperature.

Quickly pour the hot oil over the spring onion mixture. Be careful, as the oil will bubble furiously when it hits the vegetables! Stir to combine, then leave to cool.

Once cool, decant into a sterilized glass jar to store.

The following recipes use this ginger spring onion sauce:

Spring Onion, Ginger and Chicken Noodle Salad (page 65)

Ginger Spring Onion Beansprouts (page 103)

Prawns with Spring Onions, Ginger and Tomato (page 202)

TOMATO SAMBAL

Makes 300g (10½oz)

This is a brilliant sambal that I will take any day over Sriracha, or even my beloved Maggi Garlic Chilli Sauce. It is a perfect balance of spicy, sweet and tangy. The best thing is that it comes together extremely easily and quickly, and also keeps for months in the fridge!

150g (5½oz) fresh red chillies (serrano)
3 garlic cloves
60ml (¼ cup) vegetable oil
3 tbsp tomato purée (paste)
1½ tsp table salt
4½ tbsp dark brown sugar
80ml (⅓ cup) water

Blitz the chillies, garlic and oil using a handheld stick blender, or a high-speed blender like a Nutribullet, to a fine purée.

Heat a small, non-stick saucepan over a medium heat. Add the chilli-garlic mixture to the pan and stir-fry for 10 minutes, turning the heat down a little if it starts to splutter too much.

Add the tomato purée, salt, sugar and water, and stir-fry for 2 minutes just to dissolve everything. Remove from the heat and leave to cool.

Once cool, decant into a sterilized glass jar to store.

The following recipes use this tomato sambal:

Spicy Glass Noodle and Prawn Salad (page 55)

Beef and Tomato Rice (page 66)

Braised Vermicelli with Chinese Mushrooms (page 69)

Aubergines in Spicy Yellow Bean Sauce (page 106)

Tomato Eggs with Oyster Sauce (page 117)

SAMBAL TUMIS CHILLI SAUCE

Makes 220g (7¾oz)

Sadly, you will not yet find sambal tumis in Western supermarkets. *Tumis* means to 'fry off', so sambal tumis simply means a cooked sambal that includes shallots/onion carefully sautéed until sweet and fragrant. While writing this book, I did at first try to make do with Thai red curry paste and other chilli sauces/oils, but there are many Malaysian recipes for which only a great sambal tumis will do! You will always find a small Kilner jar of this sambal tumis in my fridge, ready to zhuzh up a few basic ingredients into something special in minutes. It keeps refrigerated for months.

110ml (scant ½ cup) vegetable oil
2 tbsp dark brown sugar
1 tbsp tamarind paste
1 tbsp fish sauce

Spice Paste
100g (3½oz) fresh red chillies
   (serrano), roughly chopped
1 small onion (150g/5½oz),
   roughly chopped
10 garlic cloves
2 makrut lime leaves, stems
   removed

Blitz the spice paste ingredients using a handheld stick blender, or a high-speed blender like a Nutribullet, to a fine purée.

Heat the oil in a large, non-stick saucepan over a medium heat. Stir-fry the spice paste for 10 minutes, turning the heat down to medium-low in the last few minutes if it is sticking.

Add the sugar, tamarind paste and fish sauce, stir to combine and stir-fry for another minute. Remove from the heat and leave to cool.

Once cool, decant into a sterilized glass jar to store.

The following recipes use this sambal tumis chilli sauce:

Prawn and Tomato
Noodles (page 39)

Spam Egg Fried Rice
(page 59)

Sambal Tenderstem
Broccoli (page 100)

Sambal Baked Eggs
(page 120)

Hannah's Lazy Chilli
Chicken (page 148)

Sambal Skate Wing
(page 182)

RICE, NOODLES AND PASTA

SPICY SARDINE LINGUINE

Serves 2

The original inspiration for this dish comes from one of my favourite Malaysian curry puff fillings. Malaysians have a fondness for British canned goods. It just takes a few extra store-cupboard ingredients to ramp up a couple of cans of sardines in tomato sauce. Dinner will also be on the table in under 30 minutes. If you don't feel like eating pasta, the spiced sardines are also extremely good on buttered toast or just with rice!

½ tsp table salt, or to taste, plus extra for salting the cooking water

200g (7oz) linguine

3 tbsp vegetable oil

1 small onion (150g/5½oz), finely chopped

1–2 fresh red chillies (serrano), depending on how much you like your chillies, finely sliced

2 x 95g (3½oz) cans of sardines in tomato sauce

1 tbsp Malaysian Adabi meat curry powder (if you don't have Adabi curry powder, combine ¾ tsp chilli powder, ¾ tsp ground coriander, ¾ tsp ground turmeric, ¼ tsp finely ground black pepper and ¼ tsp ground cumin)

2 tbsp tomato purée (paste)

½ tsp white sugar, or to taste

15g (½oz) bunch of fresh coriander (cilantro), roughly chopped, stems and all (optional)

½–1 lime, for squeezing

Bring a large pan of heavily salted water (like the sea) to a rolling boil and start cooking the linguine first, according to the packet instructions, as the sauce comes together very quickly.

Heat the oil in a non-stick wok or large saucepan over a medium-high heat. Stir-fry the onion with the chilli until the edges of the onions start to turn translucent, around 2 minutes.

Empty both sardine cans into the wok before adding the curry powder, tomato purée, ½ teaspoon of salt and the sugar. Stir-fry the mixture for a minute, mashing up the sardines as you do.

Add the coriander and a ladleful of the pasta cooking water. Stir to combine, then turn off the heat.

Once the linguine has cooked, drain it before adding it to the wok with the sauce. Stir thoroughly. Check for seasoning and add more salt and/or sugar as desired.

Squeeze over lime juice to taste just before eating.

Pictured on pages 32–33.

CHICKEN, BACON AND MUSHROOM RICE

Serves 4–6

One of my favourite dim sum dishes is *lor mai gai* ('sticky rice chicken') – glorious, steaming, lotus-leaf-wrapped parcels of glutinous rice with chicken, Chinese mushrooms and Chinese sausage. My interpretation uses good old jasmine rice and more easily available pancetta cubes or bacon. It's achingly good comfort food and a one-pot wonder to boot!

8 dried shiitake mushrooms
 (around 24g/1oz)
5 garlic cloves
4 tbsp vegetable oil
75g (2½oz) cubed pancetta,
 unsmoked bacon lardons,
 or finely sliced rashers of
 unsmoked streaky bacon
1 medium onion (200g/7oz),
 finely chopped
500g (1lb 2oz) skinless,
 boneless chicken thighs, cut
 into 3 x 1cm (1½ x ½in) pieces
400g (14oz/2 cups) jasmine rice,
 washed until the water runs
 clear, then thoroughly drained
 through a fine-mesh strainer

Seasoning
2 tbsp premium oyster sauce
2 pinches of ground white pepper
¼ tsp white sugar
2 tbsp light soy sauce
1 tbsp dark soy sauce
1 tsp pure sesame oil
¼ tsp five-spice
½ tsp table salt

To serve
4 spring onions (scallions),
 finely sliced
Tomato Sambal (page 28),
 or other chilli sauce/oil of
 your choice

Place the dried mushrooms in a bowl and rehydrate in 400ml (1¾ cups) just-boiled water for at least 30 minutes.

Drain the mushrooms well, reserving the soaking liquid in a measuring jug (cup). Add more water to bring the total amount of liquid to 840ml (3⅓ cups).

Discard the mushroom stalks. Finely chop the garlic and the mushroom caps using a small food processor.

Mix the seasoning ingredients in a bowl and set aside.

Heat the oil in a large casserole dish (Dutch oven) over a medium-high heat.

Stir-fry the pancetta or bacon for 3 minutes, then add the onion and stir-fry for 3 minutes until translucent. Add the garlic and mushroom mix and stir-fry for 3½ minutes. Add the chicken and stir-fry for 3 minutes. If the chicken is sticking to the dish, you can add a small splash of the soaking liquid (no more than 2½ tablespoons) to deglaze. Add the seasoning and soaking liquid, being careful not to pour in the dregs of mushroom dirt, then add the rice and stir well to thoroughly combine. Cover with the lid and bring to the boil over a high heat. As soon as it comes to the boil, reduce the heat to the lowest possible level and leave to simmer, covered, for 30 minutes.

After this time, turn off the heat and leave for 5 minutes.

Sprinkle the sliced spring onions on top and serve with a chilli condiment of your choice.

Pictured on pages 36–37.

PRAWN AND TOMATO NOODLES

Serves 2

I love Indian-Muslim *mee goreng mamak*, it's a lovely, stir-fried noodle dish to have up your sleeve. Fresh tomatoes must be used rather than canned, so I like to make this simplified version when I have some sad old tomatoes crying out to be used up. The peanuts add a textural contrast to the soft noodles. I always have a bag of raw, deshelled and deveined prawns (shrimp) in my freezer ready to dip into. They are also much cheaper than buying raw prawns from the supermarket chiller section.

3 tbsp vegetable oil
3 garlic cloves, minced
100g (3½oz) fresh tomatoes (whatever you have: salad tomatoes, cherry tomatoes, etc.), roughly chopped
½ tbsp Malaysian Adabi meat curry powder (if you don't have Adabi curry powder, combine ½ tsp chilli powder, ½ tsp ground coriander, ½ tsp ground turmeric, ¼ tsp finely ground black pepper and ¼ tsp ground cumin)
300g (10½oz) fresh egg noodles
200g (7oz) choi sum, cut into 5cm (2in) pieces
200g (7oz) raw, deshelled and deveined king prawns (jumbo shrimp), defrosted weight, if frozen – butterfly the prawns if they're very large (like the ones pictured) so that they cook quicker
2 eggs

Seasoning
2 tbsp kecap manis sweet soy sauce
1½ tbsp light soy sauce
2 tbsp ketchup (I use Heinz)
1 tbsp Sambal Tumis (page 29) or chilli sauce of your choice
½ tsp white sugar

To serve
handful of dry roasted, slightly salted peanuts, lightly crushed in a pestle and mortar (optional)
2 spring onions (scallions), finely sliced
2 fresh red chillies, finely sliced

Mix the seasoning ingredients in a bowl and set aside.

Heat the oil in a non-stick wok over a medium-high heat. Stir-fry the garlic, tomatoes and curry powder for 1 minute, then add the noodles, choi sum and seasoning mix, and stir-fry for 4 minutes.

Add the prawns and stir-fry for 2 minutes.

Push the contents to the side of the wok, leaving a small corner empty. Crack your eggs into this empty corner, leave for 15 seconds, then gently scramble before incorporating into the noodles. Stir-fry for 1 more minute.

Garnish with the lightly crushed peanuts, spring onions and chillies before serving.

FIVE-SPICE RAGU

Serves 4

A fragrant, comforting dish, I think of this as a Chinese-style ragu with five-spice and star anise. The beauty of this recipe is that you can use any minced (ground) meat you like to suit whoever you are feeding. My mother usually cooks this with pork mince and serves it with farfalle pasta, but it would work equally as well with chicken, turkey, beef or even Quorn (soya) mince. If you prefer, you can just eat the ragu with rice.

salt, for the cooking water
400g (14oz) farfalle or any other pasta of your choice
100ml (scant ½ cup) vegetable oil
1 small onion (150g/5½oz), quartered, then finely sliced
1 star anise
6 garlic cloves, minced
250ml (generous 1 cup) water
500g (1lb 2oz) minced (ground) pork (I tend to use pork mince with the highest fat content I can find, as fat means flavour!)
150g (5½oz) frozen peas

Seasoning
2 tsp cornflour (cornstarch) mixed with 2 tsp water
4 tbsp light soy sauce
½ tbsp dark soy sauce
3 tbsp sesame oil
½ tsp ground cinnamon
½ tsp five-spice
1 tsp white sugar
½ tsp ground white pepper

To serve
2 fresh red chillies, finely sliced
small handful of fresh coriander (cilantro) leaves, or 2 spring onions (scallions), finely sliced

Bring a large pan of heavily salted water (like the sea) to a rolling boil and start cooking the pasta first, according to the packet instructions, as the sauce comes together very quickly.

Mix all the seasoning ingredients together in a bowl, making sure to make up the cornflour-water mixture first.

Heat the oil in a non-stick wok or large saucepan over a high heat. Stir-fry the onion with the star anise until the edges of the onions start to turn translucent, around 2 minutes.

Add the garlic and stir-fry quickly for a minute until just starting to colour.

Add the seasoning mix, water, pork mince and peas. Bring to the boil, then gently simmer over a low heat for 5 minutes. Turn off the heat.

Once the pasta has cooked, drain it before adding it to the wok with the ragu. Stir thoroughly, then taste and adjust the seasoning if needed.

Garnish with the chillies and coriander or finely sliced spring onions before serving.

UDON WITH DARK SOY AND BACON

Serves 4

This gem of a dish is based on Kuala Lumpur *Hokkien chow mein*, which I'm sure is a derivative of another Malaysian classic, *char kway teow*. *Hokkien chow mein* is usually fried in lard and comes with delicious lardons of pork fat. My version just uses cubes of pancetta/bacon for simplicity. The combination of the bacon with dark soy sauce, oyster sauce and kecap manis is pretty epic! I like to add plenty of vegetables when cooking at home, making this a more balanced meal than what you might typically find at Malaysian hawker centres. A key component to any fried noodle dish is the *wok hei*, 'breath of the wok'. Removing the cooked vegetables before proceeding to cook the noodles makes sure that your wok isn't overcrowded and stays nice and hot.

4 tbsp vegetable oil
75g (2½oz) cubed pancetta, unsmoked bacon lardons, or finely sliced rashers of unsmoked streaky bacon
4 garlic cloves, minced
600g (1lb 5oz) choi sum, ends trimmed, then chopped into 2.5cm (1in) pieces
¼ tsp table salt
600g (1lb 5oz) ready-to-eat udon noodles
400g (14oz) ready-cooked and peeled cold-water prawns (shrimp) or brown (miniature) shrimp (fully defrosted, if frozen, and excess water gently squeezed out)
Tomato Sambal (page 28), Sambal Tumis (page 29), or other chilli sauce/oil of your choice, to serve

Seasonings
2 tbsp dark soy sauce
1 tbsp premium oyster sauce
1 tbsp kecap manis sweet soy sauce
pinch of ground white pepper

Heat 3 tablespoons of the oil in a large non-stick wok over a high heat. Stir-fry the pancetta/bacon for 2 minutes, then add the garlic and stir-fry for 10 seconds.

Add the choi sum and salt, and stir-fry for 3½ minutes. Transfer the contents of the wok to a clean bowl.

Add the remaining tablespoon of oil to the wok, then add the noodles and seasonings. Stir-fry for 3 minutes.

Add the prawns and stir-fry for 2 minutes, then return the reserved choi sum mixture back to the wok. Stir to combine, then turn off the heat.

Serve immediately with the chilli condiment of your choice.

ONE-POT CHICKEN RICE

Serves 4

Hainanese chicken rice is a classic staple in Malaysian cuisine; however, the traditional method does take some commitment to poach an entire chicken, pass it through iced water before chopping it up into more manageable pieces. I've turned it into a much simpler one-pot dish, which satisfactorily scratches the itch for Hainanese chicken rice when it arises, but I don't have the headspace to deal with the full-on traditional method! I always have a block of butter in a butter dish sitting on my kitchen counter so that I have soft butter ready to add to my cooking by the tablespoon. This dish is very tasty just eaten by itself, but if you need more sauces, the Ginger Spring Onion Sauce (page 27) and/or the Tomato Sambal (page 28) will do nicely.

2 tbsp salted butter

½ small onion (75g/2½oz), finely diced

4 garlic cloves, minced

400g (14oz/2 cups) jasmine rice, washed until the water runs clear, then thoroughly drained through a fine-mesh strainer

½ tbsp table salt

2.5cm (1in) piece of ginger, cut into thin slices

1 tbsp pure sesame oil

400g (14oz) chicken breast, cut into 3 x 1cm (1½ x ½in) pieces (you can use pre-diced breast, but I find the pieces a bit too big for my liking!)

800ml (3½ cups) chicken stock (fine to make it up with a chicken stock/bouillon cube)

To serve

15g (½oz) bunch of fresh coriander (cilantro), roughly chopped, stems and all

2 spring onions (scallions), finely sliced

Ginger Spring Onion Sauce (page 27), optional

Tomato Sambal (page 28), or other chilli sauce/oil of your choice

Add the butter to a large casserole dish (Dutch oven) and melt over a medium-high heat. Once melted, add the onion and garlic, and stir-fry for 2 minutes. Add the rice, salt, ginger, sesame oil, chicken and stock, and stir well.

Turn the heat up to high and bring to the boil, stirring often – this will take around 3–5 minutes. Cover with the lid, reduce the heat to the lowest level and simmer for 30 minutes.

After this time, turn off the heat and leave to rest for 10 minutes.

Add the chopped coriander and stir through the rice, then sprinkle over the spring onions. If desired, serve with ginger spring onion sauce and the chilli condiment of your choice on the side.

SPAGHETTI WITH BROCCOLI AND SHRIMP PASTE

Serves 4

During the COVID pandemic lockdowns, I hunted for easy recipes that my husband could make for us. Jamie Oliver's recipe for farfalle with broccoli, anchovies and chilli fitted the bill perfectly. Jamie's original is still very much in my husband's weekend cooking rotation. This version was born when we were out of anchovies one weekend. I suggested that he use shrimp paste instead and, lo and behold, it worked a treat! We also added some lime juice to lift the shrimp paste's deep savouriness.

1 head of broccoli (400g/14oz)
salt, for the cooking water
4 tbsp vegetable oil
2 garlic cloves, minced
1 tbsp dried chilli (red pepper) flakes
½ tbsp shrimp paste (or substitute 2 tbsp fish sauce)
450g (1lb) dried spaghetti
1 lime, for squeezing

Remove the florets from the broccoli and finely chop them, then trim, peel and finely chop the stalks.

Bring a large pan of heavily salted water (like the sea) to a rolling boil ready to start cooking the spaghetti later.

At the same time, heat the oil in a non-stick wok over a medium heat. Fry the broccoli, garlic and chilli flakes for about 10 minutes, with the lid on, stirring every few minutes. Towards the end of the cooking time, add the shrimp paste, stir and turn off the heat.

While the broccoli is cooking, start cooking the spaghetti, according to the packet instructions.

When the spaghetti is nearly ready, add a ladleful of the pasta cooking water to the broccoli mix.

Drain the spaghetti. Turn the heat under the broccoli mix back to medium-high and add the spaghetti to the pan. Stir to mix everything together.

Serve with a squeeze of lime juice, to taste.

FRIED VERMICELLI WITH DRIED SHRIMP AND CHICKEN

Serves 4

Malaysians are very fond of surf and turf in our cooking. All sorts of dried seafood add a saline depth to many meat and/or vegetable stir-fries; e.g. *ikan bilis* (dried anchovies), scallops, oysters, cuttlefish – you name it, we will dry it! These are comforting Chinese-style fried noodles with a gorgeous umami backbone of dried shrimp. You don't need much of these little beauties, as a little goes a long way. The technique of removing the cooked vegetables from the wok before proceeding to cook the chicken and then the noodles makes sure that your wok stays nice and hot, and also that you don't over/undercook your vegetables.

375–400g (13–14oz) thin rice vermicelli noodles, steeped in cold water for 30 minutes until pliable

3 tbsp (23g/1oz) dried shrimp, soaked in 100ml (scant ½ cup) just-boiled hot water for at least 30 minutes

4 tbsp vegetable oil

4 garlic cloves, minced

1 head of Chinese leaves (600g/1lb 5oz), cut in half, core removed, then each half cut in half again before being chopped into 1cm (½in) slices

½ tsp table salt

500g (1lb 2oz) skinless, boneless chicken thighs, cut into 3 x 1cm (1½ x ½in) strips

2 tbsp premium oyster sauce

1 tbsp dark soy sauce

1 tbsp pure sesame oil

2 pinches of ground white pepper

To serve

6 bird's eye chillies, finely sliced (optional)

30g (1oz) fresh coriander (cilantro), roughly chopped, stems and all (optional)

Drain the vermicelli noodles ready for use.

Drain the dried shrimp, but keep the soaking water.

Heat 2 tablespoons of the oil in a large non-stick wok over a high heat. Stir-fry the dried shrimp for 2 minutes, then add the garlic and stir-fry for 10 seconds.

Add the Chinese leaves and salt, and stir-fry for 5 minutes. Transfer the contents of the wok to a clean bowl.

Add the remaining 2 tablespoons of oil to the wok along with the chicken. Stir-fry for 5 minutes. In the last minute, add the oyster sauce and continue to cook.

Add the dark soy sauce to the reserved shrimp soaking water.

Add the vermicelli noodles to the wok and pour the soy shrimp water around them. Add the sesame oil and white pepper, and stir-fry for 8 minutes.

Add the Chinese leaf mixture back to the wok. If using, garnish with chillies and coriander now. Stir to combine and serve.

DIY 'INDOMIE'

Serves 2

All South East Asians will be familiar with Indomie *mi goreng* – thin, springy, instant noodles mixed with sachets of unmistakable sweet/savoury flavour. Although you will find Indomie in many Western supermarkets nowadays, I sometimes like making my own, as it is mind-bogglingly simple and doesn't contain any extra preservatives. Shallot oil is the Most Valuable Player of this recipe – you can't make it without – and you must have a fried egg with crispy edges!

125g (4½oz) dried fine egg noodles (2 pucks)
Shallot Oil (page 26)
4 tbsp kecap manis sweet soy sauce
150g (5½oz) beansprouts
2 eggs

To serve
a few stalks of fresh coriander (cilantro), including stems (optional)
2 spring onions (scallions), finely sliced
Tomato Sambal (page 28), or other sharp chilli sauce or chilli oil

Cover the egg noodles with just-boiled hot water. Drain after 3 minutes and rinse thoroughly under cold running water to wash away the excess starch.

Add 3 tablespoons of pure oil from the shallot oil and 2 tablespoons of the fried shallots drained from the oil to a non-stick wok set over a medium-high heat.

Add the noodles and kecap manis, and stir-fry for 5 minutes, leaving for 20 seconds every now and then to allow the bottom to char.

Add the beansprouts and stir-fry for another 2 minutes. Transfer the noodles and beansprouts to two plates.

Using the same wok, fry the eggs, then place on top of the noodles.

Tear up the coriander and sprinkle over the dish together with the spring onions. Serve immediately with the chilli condiment of your choice.

CONGEE WITH CHICKEN AND GINGER

Serves 4

My mum would make this whenever I was ill, so it's now my go-to whenever anyone in my family is feeling under the weather. This congee is particularly restorative and easy to digest. Whoever is eating it can tailor their bowl with as little or as much spring onion (scallion), shallot oil, sesame oil and/or soy sauce as they like! If you don't have shallot oil, it will still be gorgeous served simply with sesame oil and soy sauce.

4 skinless, bone-in chicken thighs (approximately 500g/1lb 2oz)
2 litres (8¾ cups) water
250g (9oz/1¼ cups) white rice
1 chicken stock (bouillon) cube
2.5cm (1in) piece of ginger, cut into thin slices
2 carrots, halved lengthways and sliced into 1cm (½in) semicircles
½ tsp table salt
¼ tsp ground white pepper
2 spring onions (scallions), finely sliced into rounds
small handful of fresh coriander (cilantro) leaves (optional)

To serve
Shallot Oil (page 26)
pure sesame oil
light soy sauce

Add the chicken and water to a large casserole dish (Dutch oven) or stock pot and bring to the boil. Turn off the heat and skim off all the impurities at the top.

Add the rice, stock cube, ginger, carrots, salt and pepper to the pot and bring back to the boil, then reduce the heat to the lowest possible level and simmer, covered, for 20 minutes.

Remove the lid and cook for a further 15 minutes, stirring every few minutes, especially towards the end, to prevent the rice from sticking to the bottom of the pot.

Turn off the heat and remove the pieces of chicken from the pot to a plate to cool. After around 15 minutes, once the chicken is cool to the touch, remove the meat from the bones and shred. Add the shredded chicken back to the pot.

Divide the congee between four bowls and sprinkle with the spring onions and coriander, if using. Serve alongside shallot oil, sesame oil and light soy sauce so that each person can season their bowl to their own taste.

Pictured on pages 52–53.

SPICY GLASS NOODLE AND PRAWN SALAD

Serves 4–6

Kerabu is an umbrella term in Malay denoting a vibrant salad of vegetables and herbs, dressed with a fiery sambal, shrimp paste and lime to bring everything together. The dressing is spicy, sharp and smells wonderful from all the herbs. You might also find *kerabu* noodle salads. This is my very easy version, perfect for hot summer days as it doesn't involve any cooking. I've substituted canned anchovies (use the best you can afford) in place of shrimp paste to avoid having to toast the shrimp paste. Coincidentally, when I blitzed up the first test of this dressing, it smelt very much like *cincalok*, another Malaysian speciality of fermented krill mixed with shallots and chillies. A traditional *kerabu* salad will always include laksa leaves or hot mint, but I know these are relatively tricky to find in the diaspora, so I have used a mixture of herbs more commonly found in Western supermarkets. I find that the basil goes a little way towards the fragrant pepperiness of hot mint.

150g (5½oz) mung bean glass noodles, soaked in just-boiled water for at least 10 minutes
30g (1oz) fresh basil, leaves picked
30g (1oz) bunch of mint, leaves picked and roughly chopped
30g (1oz) bunch of fresh coriander (cilantro), roughly chopped, stems and all
300g (10½oz) pre-cooked, peeled small cold-water prawns (shrimp) – fully defrosted, if frozen, and excess water gently squeezed out
¾ cucumber, deseeded and cut into 1cm (½in) cubes

Dressing
2 fresh red chillies (serrano)
1 banana shallot, roughly chopped
4 fresh makrut lime leaves, stems removed
50g (1¾oz) canned anchovy fillets, including the oil
juice of 1 lime
1 tbsp dark brown sugar
3 tbsp Tomato Sambal (page 28), or other chilli sauce (such as Maggi garlic chilli sauce or Sriracha)
1 tbsp fish sauce
1 tsp tamarind paste
3 tbsp extra-virgin olive oil

Blitz the dressing ingredients in a small food processor.

Drain the mung bean noodles and place into a large mixing bowl. Roughly tear the basil leaves into the noodles.

To allow for the flavours to come together, thoroughly mix in the remaining ingredients along with the dressing at least 15 minutes before you want to eat this salad.

Note: If making this recipe in advance of when you want to eat it, hold off from adding the cucumber until 15 minutes before serving. The cucumber releases water after a while, which will make for a very watery salad!

Pictured on pages 56–57.

SPAM EGG FRIED RICE

Serves 2

East Asians generally have no qualms at all about Spam, as it is packed full of flavour and is a super-quick injection of salt, fat and protein. We love adding it to all sorts of things – my favourite is having it with fried rice. It is vitally important that all your rice and vegetable preparation is done before you start to cook this. Keep the wok on the largest burner over the highest heat for the entire process. Please use the original, full-fat, full-salt Spam – don't be conned by the lesser versions! I also like to add finely chopped bird's eye chillies at the end, for extra heat.

1 tbsp vegetable oil
200g (7oz) Spam, cut into 1cm (½in) cubes
2 spring onions (scallions), finely sliced
2 garlic cloves, minced
400g (14oz) leftover rice, which ideally has first been warmed up in the microwave
1 tbsp kecap manis sweet soy sauce
1 tbsp Sambal Tumis (page 29), or other chilli sauce/oil
pinch of ground black pepper
100g (3½oz) frozen peas
2 eggs

To serve (optional)
handful of fresh coriander (cilantro) leaves, roughly chopped
2 bird's eye chillies, finely sliced

Heat the oil in a non-stick wok over a medium heat. Add the Spam and evenly spread it out around the wok. Leave for 30 seconds or so to allow it to render, then stir-fry for 3 minutes until evenly coloured.

Add the spring onions and garlic, increase the heat to medium-high and stir-fry for 30 seconds.

Add the rice, kecap manis, sambal tumis and pepper. Mix well and stir-fry for 3 minutes, if the rice has been warmed up in the microwave (or 6 minutes, if starting from cold).

Add the peas and stir-fry for 2 minutes.

Push the contents to the side of the wok, leaving a small corner empty. Crack your eggs into this empty corner, leave for 15 seconds, then stir to roughly scramble before incorporating into the rice. Stir-fry for 1 more minute.

Serve immediately, garnished with coriander and scattered with the bird's eye chillies, if using.

GREEN PASTA WITH CHILLI AND CUMIN

Serves 4

A brilliant Julius Roberts recipe introduced me to the phenomenon of green pasta. This is my take on it, adding a good dose of cumin as I absolutely love *saag aloo*. Feel free to adjust the chilli content, depending on how spicy you like things!

salt, for the cooking water

400g (14oz) pasta of your choice (I like fusilli for this recipe, as its ridges take on the green sauce beautifully)

3 tbsp vegetable oil

4 garlic cloves, minced

1 fresh red chilli (serrano), finely sliced

1 tsp ground cumin

200g (7oz) kale or cavolo nero, stems removed, roughly chopped (or you can use spinach instead)

mild Cheddar or Parmesan, grated (shredded), to serve

Bring a large pan of heavily salted water (like the sea) to a rolling boil and start cooking the pasta first, according to the packet instructions, as the sauce comes together very quickly.

While the pasta is cooking, heat the oil in a non-stick medium saucepan over a medium-high heat. Fry off the garlic, chilli and cumin for 1 minute, then add the kale and 2 ladlefuls of the pasta cooking water to the pan. Stir to combine and cook, covered with a lid, for 4 minutes, stirring halfway through.

Using a stick blender, or a high-speed blender like a Nutribullet, blitz the contents of the saucepan into a sauce.

Drain the pasta before putting it back into the pan in which it cooked. Add the green sauce and stir well.

Serve with generous amounts of grated cheese.

ABC SOUP WITH MACARONI

Serves 4

'ABC soup' is very popular in East Asian cultures, and certainly in Malaysia. Perhaps this name came about because the soup is so straightforward to prepare – as easy as ABC. Or potentially because its ingredients are full of vitamins A (carrots), B (potatoes) and C (tomatoes and potatoes). Traditional ABC soup is usually cooked without pasta and eaten with rice. Behold my version of a comforting, nourishing Chinese chicken noodle soup! I like dipping mouthfuls of potatoes and/or carrots into chilli-laden soy sauce before eating.

4 skinless, bone-in chicken
   thighs (500g/1lb 2oz)
1.5 litres (6½ cups) water
1 small onion (150g/5½oz),
   peeled and cut into quarters
1 carrot, halved lengthways and
   cut into 2cm (¾in) semicircles
1 celery stick, cut into 2cm (¾in)
   pieces (optional)
2 tsp table salt
2 pinches of ground white pepper
1 potato (300g/10½oz), peeled
   and cut into 2cm (¾in) chunks
3–4 fresh tomatoes (200g/7oz),
   quartered
50g (1¾oz) macaroni

To serve
8 bird's eye chillies, finely sliced
light soy sauce

Add the chicken and water to a large casserole dish (Dutch oven) or stock pot and bring to the boil. Turn off the heat and skim off all the impurities at the top.

Add the onion, carrot, celery, salt and pepper to the pot and bring back to the boil before reducing to the lowest simmer, uncovered, so that the surface is just gently blipping away for 1 hour.

After this time, remove the chicken from the pot to cool and add the potato, tomatoes and macaroni. Bring back to the boil before turning back down to the lowest simmer for 30 minutes.

Once the chicken pieces are cool to the touch, strip the meat from the bones and add back to the pot.

Turn off the heat. Using a pair of tongs, pinch all the skins away from the flesh of the tomatoes, one by one, and discard.

Serve with the bird's eye chillies in soy sauce on the side.

SPRING ONION, GINGER AND CHICKEN NOODLE SALAD

Serves 4

During a heatwave, I love a noodle salad served cold or at room temperature. This joyous dish, inspired by Chinese spring onion noodles, is super simple to put together, especially if you already have cooked chicken. I like to buy ready-cooked, plain roasted chicken thighs from the supermarket rotisserie, and then strip the meat and skin, ready for a low-effort, no-cook dinner! I also often roast a few extra chicken thighs before shredding the meat and freezing it, so I have ready-to-go cooked chicken whenever I need it. You'll need to make one batch of the Ginger Spring Onion Sauce on page 27 before starting, which can be done days in advance.

190–200g (6¾–7oz) dried fine
   egg noodles (3 pucks)
200–250g (7–9oz) chicken
   meat, stripped and shredded
   from 4 store-bought rotisserie
   chicken thighs or leftover
   roasted chicken thighs
180–200g (6¼–7oz) baby
   spinach, washed and dried
15g (½oz) fresh coriander
   (cilantro), roughly chopped,
   stems and all

Dressing
1 batch of Ginger Spring Onion
   Sauce (page 27)
2 tsp honey
3 tbsp rice vinegar
¼ tsp table salt
3 pinches of ground white pepper

To serve (optional)
8 bird's eye chillies, finely sliced
light soy sauce

Cover the egg noodles with just-boiled hot water. Drain after 4 minutes and rinse thoroughly under cold running water to wash away the excess starch.

In a large mixing bowl, mix together the dressing ingredients.

Add the chicken, spinach, drained noodles and coriander to the dressing. Mix thoroughly and serve alongside bird's eye chillies in soy sauce.

BEEF AND TOMATO RICE

Serves 4–6

The origins of Malay *nasi tomato* must have been Indian biryani, with the use of fragrant spices during the cooking process. You will often find tomato rice at Malay feasts accompanying rich curries and stews like *rendang*. I've used the idea of *nasi tomato* but zhuzhed it up with minced (ground) beef for protein and peas for a more balanced one-pot meal – sort of like fried rice that you don't have to fry! Fresh tomatoes add a fabulous tang at the end. Please do not use canned tomatoes for this recipe.

1 small onion (150g/5½oz), roughly chopped

3 garlic cloves

2.5cm (½in) piece of ginger, peeled and roughly chopped

3 tbsp salted butter

500g (1lb 2oz) minced (ground) beef

400g (14oz/2 cups) white rice, jasmine or basmati, washed until the water runs clear, then thoroughly drained through a sieve

2 tbsp tomato purée (paste)

2 tsp table salt

800ml (3½ cups) water

1 star anise

3 cloves

1 cassia bark stick or ½ cinnamon stick

2 cardamom pods, gently bashed with a pestle to crack the skin

150g (5½oz) frozen peas

300–400g (10½–14oz) fresh tomatoes, deseeded and chopped into 1cm (½in) cubes

15g (½oz) bunch of fresh coriander (cilantro), roughly chopped, stems and all (optional)

2 tbsp fried shallots drained from Shallot Oil (page 26)

1–2 tbsp Tomato Sambal (page 28) or any other chilli sauce (depending on how much chilli you like)

Finely chop the onion, garlic cloves and ginger in a small food processor.

Warm the butter in a large casserole dish (Dutch oven) over a medium heat. Add the onion-garlic-ginger mixture and stir-fry for 2 minutes. Add a couple of splashes of water if the mixture starts to stick – no more than 100ml (scant ½ cup) in total.

Add the beef and stir-fry for 5 minutes.

Add the rice, tomato purée, salt, measured water, star anise, cloves, cassia bark or cinnamon, cardamom pods and peas. Stir, cover with the lid and bring to the boil, then reduce to the lowest possible heat and simmer for 30 minutes.

Turn off the heat and leave to rest for 10 minutes.

Stir through the tomatoes, coriander (if using), fried shallots and tomato sambal before serving.

BRAISED VERMICELLI WITH CHINESE MUSHROOMS

Serves 4

I drew inspiration from two places for this super-easy, one-pot dish: a Chinese sweet potato noodle dish called 'ants climbing a tree' and Malaysian Nyonya *chap chye*, which is a braised vegetable stew with bean thread noodles. My version simply uses rice vermicelli noodles, as they are easily found in Western supermarkets nowadays. You can substitute the minced (ground) pork for chicken mince, Quorn (soya) or finely chopped firm tofu, if desired. Most of the work is in the pre-soaking of ingredients and vegetable preparation, which I tend to do while my son is having his nap.

375–400g (13–14oz) thin rice vermicelli noodles, steeped in cold water for 30 minutes until pliable

8 dried shiitake mushrooms (around 24g/1oz), soaked in 250ml (generous 1 cup) just-boiled hot water for at least 30 minutes

1 small onion (150g/5½oz), roughly chopped

2.5cm (1in) piece of ginger, roughly chopped

3 garlic cloves

500g (1lb 2oz) minced (ground) pork

3 tbsp vegetable oil

1 head of Chinese leaves (600g/1lb 5oz), cut in half, core removed, then each half cut in half again before being chopped into 1cm (½in) slices

2 tbsp yellow bean sauce or 1 tbsp white shiro miso paste

3 tbsp light soy sauce

Seasonings

1 tbsp Shaoxing rice wine or Harvey's Bristol Cream sherry

2 tbsp Tomato Sambal (page 28) or any other chilli sauce that you have available

1 tbsp pure sesame oil

2 tsp cornflour (cornstarch)

2 tsp white sugar

pinch of ground white pepper

To serve

2 spring onions (scallions), finely sliced

large handful of fresh coriander (cilantro) leaves, roughly chopped (optional)

Drain the vermicelli noodles ready for use.

Drain the mushrooms, keeping the soaking liquid for later. Discard the mushroom stalks and finely slice the caps.

Finely chop the onion, ginger and garlic cloves in a small food processor.

Thoroughly mix the seasonings through the pork mince.

When ready to cook, heat the oil in a non-stick wok over a high heat. Fry the onion-garlic-ginger mixture for 3 minutes, then add the seasoned pork mince and the mushrooms and stir-fry for 5 minutes until the mince is cooked.

Add the Chinese leaves and yellow bean sauce or miso paste, and stir-fry for 2 minutes until the edges of the leaves turn translucent.

Add the vermicelli noodles, soy sauce and reserved mushroom soaking water to the pan (leave the dregs, as you don't want the sediment). Stir-fry for around 3 minutes until the noodles have just absorbed the moisture. Taste and add more of any of the seasonings, as desired.

Serve warm garnished with the sliced spring onions and chopped coriander, if using.

VEG-CENTRIC AND PULSES

WATERCRESS AND ANCHOVY SOUP

Serves 4

I often make a quick soup using Malaysian dried anchovy stock. The savoury broth in this recipe comes together even quicker, as it uses canned anchovies readily available in Western supermarkets as its base. I tend to serve this soup as the vegetable component of a meal, where the other dish has a drier consistency, e.g. the Hainanese Roast Chicken (page 134). You can also substitute spinach for watercress in this recipe; just note that it'll cook much quicker than the watercress, as the soup is ready as soon as it all wilts.

2 garlic cloves, minced
50g (1¾oz) canned anchovies
   in olive oil
1 litre (4⅓ cups) water
¼ tsp table salt
320g (11¼oz) fresh watercress
   leaves, washed
2 pinches of ground white pepper

To serve
2 spring onions (scallions),
   finely sliced
1 tsp pure sesame oil (optional)

Add the garlic to a large saucepan, then pour in the entire contents of the anchovy can, including the oil. Stir-fry over a medium heat for a minute, breaking up and mashing the anchovies as you go. They will start to splutter, so you can add a splash of water to calm things down.

Add the water and salt, and bring to the boil, then add the watercress and simmer for 5 minutes, stirring every now and then, until the watercress has wilted.

Finish with white pepper. Taste and add more salt, if desired.

Use a pair of kitchen scissors to cut up the watercress in the soup to make it easier to eat. Sprinkle the spring onions and sesame oil on top to garnish and serve.

Pictured on pages 72–73.

MALAYSIAN MUSHROOM AND BEAN STEW

Serves 3–4

This is my take on Malaysian *kacang phool*, which originated from Middle Eastern *foul mudammas*, usually made with broad (fava) beans. I absolutely love canned baked beans and always have a can or two hanging around, so I've chosen to use them instead alongside chickpeas (garbanzo beans), another of my store-cupboard staples. Delicious for a weekend brunch, served with heavily buttered toast and fried eggs, sunny sides up!

1 small onion (150g/5½oz),
   roughly chopped
2 garlic cloves
1cm (½in) piece of ginger
   (15g/½oz), peeled and
   roughly chopped
400g (14oz) canned baked beans
50g (1¾oz) salted butter
1 tbsp vegetable oil
250g (9oz) baby button
   or chestnut (cremini)
   mushrooms, halved
1 tbsp Malaysian Adabi meat
   curry powder (if you don't
   have Adabi curry powder,
   combine ¾ tsp chilli powder,
   ¾ tsp ground coriander, ¾ tsp
   ground turmeric, ¼ tsp finely
   ground black pepper and
   ¼ tsp ground cumin)
1 tsp ground cumin
½ tsp coarsely ground
   black pepper
½ tsp table salt
300ml (generous 1¼ cups) water
400g (14oz) canned chickpeas
   (garbanzo beans) in salted
   water, drained and rinsed
1 lime, for squeezing

To serve
2 banana shallots, finely diced
15g (½oz) bunch of fresh
   coriander (cilantro), roughly
   chopped, stems and all
2 fresh red chillies, finely chopped

Finely chop the onion, garlic and ginger in a small food processor. Transfer the mixture to a large non-stick saucepan.

Using the same food processor bowl (no need to wash in between), blitz the whole can of baked beans to a purée.

Add the butter, oil and mushrooms to the saucepan and stir-fry with the onion mix over a medium heat for 10 minutes.

Add the curry powder, cumin, black pepper, salt and 100ml (scant ½ cup) of the water. Stir-fry for 1 minute, then add the puréed baked beans, chickpeas and the rest of the water. Bring to the boil, stirring often, then immediately remove from the heat.

Squeeze the lime over before serving with the shallots, coriander and chillies sprinkled on top.

Pictured on pages 76–77.

SAMBAL AUBERGINES AND OKRA

Serves 4

Frozen okra that has already been cut into rounds is a ready-to-go vegetable I like to always have in my freezer. This is a gorgeous dish full of chilli and *wok hei* 'breath of the wok'. Irresistible to any Malaysian, and hopefully now also irresistible to you!

1 small onion (150g/5½oz), roughly chopped

2 garlic cloves

3 fresh red chillies (serrano), roughly chopped

135ml (generous ½ cup) vegetable oil

1 aubergine (eggplant) (300g/10½oz), cut into 2.5cm (1in) chunks

¼ tsp table salt

300g (10½oz) okra, tops sliced off, cut into 2cm (¾in) pieces either on the diagonal or in rounds (frozen, pre-cut okra works perfectly here)

1 tbsp kecap manis sweet soy sauce

Finely chop the onion, garlic cloves and chillies in a small food processor.

Heat 60ml (¼ cup) of the oil in a non-stick wok over a medium-high heat and stir-fry the aubergine with ⅛ teaspoon of the salt for 3 minutes. Remove from the pan to a clean bowl or plate.

Add the rest of the vegetable oil to the wok together with the onion-chilli-garlic mixture and the remaining ⅛ teaspoon salt. Stir-fry for 10 minutes over a medium heat.

Add the okra and kecap manis, stir to combine and stir-fry for 2 minutes.

Add the aubergine back to the wok, stir to combine and serve immediately.

CREAMED SPINACH WITH DRIED SHRIMP

Serves 4

I absolutely adore creamed spinach and have added the Malaysian staples of coconut milk and dried shrimp to the traditional version. It's really useful to have frozen baby spinach in your freezer so that you can throw this side dish together any time you've forgotten to pick up fresh vegetables for dinner. Fabulous!

2 tbsp vegetable oil

1 tbsp dried shrimp, soaked in 60ml (¼ cup) just-boiled hot water for at least 30 minutes

4 garlic cloves, minced

200ml (scant 1 cup) coconut milk

½ tsp table salt

1 tsp cornflour (cornstarch) mixed with 1 tbsp water

800g (1lb 12oz) baby spinach (frozen works perfectly here)

2 pinches of ground white pepper

½ lemon, for squeezing (optional)

Heat the oil in a large saucepan over a medium heat.

Drain the dried shrimp with one hand, squeezing out as much of the water as possible, and put straight into the pan. Stir-fry for 30 seconds, then add the garlic and stir-fry for 10 seconds.

Add the coconut milk, salt and cornflour-water mixture, and stir for 20 seconds to thicken the sauce.

Add the spinach and white pepper, then stir-fry for 4 minutes over a medium-low heat to warm the spinach through.

Add a squeeze of lemon juice just before serving.

GREEN BEANS AND SOY

Serves 2

There used to be a fantastic old-school Italian restaurant called Al Fresco in Whetstone, North London, where I first tried these stir-fried green beans on the side of some veal Milanese. Theirs were very simply seasoned with salt and black pepper. My version uses light soy to great effect. You'll be surprised at how good these are!

salt, for the cooking water
200g (7oz) green beans,
    destemmed and cut into
    2.5cm (1in) pieces
1½ tbsp vegetable oil
1 small onion (150g/5½oz),
    quartered and thinly sliced
2 garlic cloves, minced
2 tbsp light soy sauce
pinch of ground white pepper

Bring a small saucepan of heavily salted water (like the sea) to the boil. Blanch the beans for 4 minutes, then drain.

Heat the oil in a large non-stick wok over a high heat and stir-fry the onion until the edges turn translucent. Add the garlic and stir-fry for 10 seconds, then add the blanched beans, soy sauce and white pepper, and stir to combine. Serve immediately.

SPRING GREENS AND CHICKPEA CURRY

Serves 4

This is a wonderfully quick curry to throw together. I choose to use Worcestershire sauce over tamarind for this curry, as the anchovy essence in the Worcestershire sauce really adds another level to the gravy. If you're vegan, feel free to just use tamarind paste, but add sugar to balance out the flavours. You can simply serve this on its own with rice, or as a side dish. It does pack a decent chilli kick, so you can use one or even no chillies at all, if you wish to make it milder.

¾ tsp table salt, plus extra for the cooking water

1 small onion (150g/5½oz), roughly chopped

2.5cm (1in) piece of ginger, peeled and roughly chopped

3 garlic cloves

2 fresh red chillies (serrano), roughly chopped (optional)

4 tbsp vegetable oil

1 tsp ground turmeric

300g (10½oz) spring greens, leaves stripped from the stalks and sliced into 1cm (½in) pieces

400g (14oz) canned chickpeas (garbanzo beans) in salted water, drained and rinsed

250ml (generous 1 cup) UHT coconut cream (usually found in a can or carton)

2 tbsp Worcestershire sauce (I use Lea & Perrins) or tamarind paste

½ tsp white sugar (only add if using tamarind paste)

Bring a large pot of heavily salted water (like the sea) to a rolling boil.

Using a food processor to save time, finely chop the onion, ginger, garlic and chillies. Transfer the mixture to a large non-stick wok, then add the oil, ¾ teaspoon salt and turmeric, and place over a medium-high heat. Stir-fry for 9 minutes, stirring frequently to avoid burning.

While the onions are cooking, add the spring greens and chickpeas to the pot of boiling water. Simmer over a medium heat for 5 minutes. Drain thoroughly.

Add the coconut cream, Worcestershire sauce and sugar to the wok. Bring to the boil, then turn off the heat. Add the spring greens and chickpeas to the sauce, stir to combine and serve.

SHRIMP PASTE FRIED CABBAGE

Serves 4

This is a homage to Lee Tiernan of Black Axe Mangal's charred hispi (sweetheart) cabbage with shrimp paste, which I'm sure in itself was a homage to the Malaysian classic of *kangkung belacan* (morning glory stir-fried with shrimp paste). Lee blanches his cabbage before finishing them off over charcoal flames. I've kept it as a wonderfully simple stir-fry.

3 tbsp oil
2 garlic cloves, minced
30g (1oz) fresh coriander (cilantro), finely chopped, stems and all
1 hispi (sweetheart) cabbage, cut into eighths, core removed, then cut into 1cm (½in) slices
2 tbsp salted butter
½ tsp shrimp paste (or substitute with 1 tsp fish sauce)

Heat the oil in a large non-stick wok over a high heat. Stir-fry the garlic and coriander for 30 seconds, then add the cabbage and stir-fry for 6 minutes, only stirring every 15 seconds or so to achieve some nice charring on the leaves.

Make a well in the centre of the cabbage. Add the butter and shrimp paste to the hole and stir-fry for 30 seconds, then stir to combine with the cabbage. Serve immediately.

CHAYOTE WITH DRIED SHRIMP AND GLASS NOODLES

Serves 4

If you see chayote (a.k.a. cho cho or chow chow) in your local supermarket or African or Asian grocer, I urge you to try it as it has a fabulous tender crispness when cooked. Alternatively, this recipe would also work just as well with Chinese leaves, courgettes (zucchini) or broccoli. Vegetables stir-fried with dried shrimp and garlic will taste like home to every Malaysian-Chinese.

2 tbsp (15g/½oz) dried shrimp, soaked in 60ml (¼ cup) just-boiled hot water for at least 30 minutes
50g (1¾oz) mung bean glass noodles, soaked in just-boiled hot water for at least 10 minutes
3 tbsp vegetable oil
2 garlic cloves, minced
2 chayote (chow chow) (about 600g/1lb 5oz), peeled, seeds removed and cut into 6cm x 5mm (2½ x ¼in) slices
¾ tsp table salt
pinch of ground white pepper

Drain the dried shrimp using one hand, squeezing out as much of the water as possible, but keep the soaking water.

Drain the glass noodles and cut into 5–7.5cm (2–3in) lengths.

Heat the oil in a large non-stick wok over a high heat. Stir-fry the drained dried shrimp for 1 minute, then add the garlic and stir-fry for another 10 seconds.

Add the chayote, salt, pepper and reserved shrimp soaking water. Stir-fry for 4 minutes, then add the glass noodles and stir-fry for a final minute. Serve immediately.

SILKEN TOFU WITH FRIED SHALLOTS, SESAME AND SOY

Serves 4

This is such an amazingly quick dish to put together. It's super-tasty and incredibly satisfying eaten on its own or just with rice. You can use either the larger blocks of tofu sold in the chiller sections of East Asian supermarkets, or the shelf-stable tofu sold in smaller cardboard cartons. To remove the shelf-stable tofu from the carton, you need to cut open both ends of the carton over the sink so that the excess water drains away, before cutting open the middle of the carton and sliding it out. You want to have as nice a block of tofu for presentation purposes, as this dish is so simple. If you haven't made the shallot oil, store-bought fried shallots and pure sesame oil will do.

1 x 480g (1lb 1oz) chilled block of silken tofu or 2 x 300g (10½oz) shelf-stable cartons
4 tbsp Shallot Oil (page 26)
3 tbsp light soy sauce
small handful of fresh coriander (cilantro), leaves picked
2 spring onions (scallions), finely sliced
1 fresh red chilli, finely sliced

Carefully place the tofu on a small lipped plate or in a shallow bowl.

Bring a steamer pan of water to the boil. It should be big enough to hold the plate or bowl with the tofu, and have a lid that is able to close flush. Steam the tofu for 12 minutes over a medium-high heat.

Once the tofu is hot, carefully drain or spoon off half of the water in the tofu plate.

Drizzle 2 tablespoons of pure oil from the shallot oil over the tofu, to reignite the oil's aroma. Drizzle over the soy sauce and sprinkle the coriander, spring onions and chilli over the tofu. Finally drizzle over 2 tablespoons of fried shallots, drained from the shallot oil, and serve immediately.

CREAMY SAVOY CABBAGE AND CELERY

Serves 4

One of my favourite Malaysian eateries is Dapur in Lamb Conduit's Passage in Holborn, London. I really enjoy their kale *masak lemak* (kale cooked in coconut milk) as part of their Malay *nasi campur* selection of economy rice dishes. I've used Savoy cabbage, as I prefer its sweetness, and have also thrown in some celery for additional depth of flavour. The celery is optional, but it is so often begging to be used after I make a batch of spaghetti bolognese. In an effort not to waste it, I usually add celery to whatever vegetable side dish I'm cooking in the following days.

3 tbsp vegetable oil
1 small onion (150g/5½oz), quartered and thinly sliced
3 celery sticks, finely sliced (optional)
1 tsp table salt
2 garlic cloves, minced
½ Savoy cabbage (about 400–450g/14oz–1lb), cut in half, core removed, cut into 1cm (½in) slices
200ml (scant 1 cup) coconut milk
200ml (scant 1 cup) water
1 tbsp light soy sauce
small handful of fresh coriander (cilantro), leaves picked, to garnish

Heat the oil in a large non-stick wok over a high heat. Stir-fry the onion, celery and salt until the edges of the onions turn translucent.

Add the garlic and stir-fry for 10 seconds, then add the cabbage, coconut milk, water and soy sauce. Stir to combine, then reduce the heat to medium, cover and simmer for 3 minutes.

Garnish with coriander and serve.

SPICED BAKED BEANS

Serves 2–3

Canned baked beans are a staple in a Malaysian pantry, due to its colonial past. I absolutely love the comforting familiarity of this dish and am known to sometimes substitute plain baked beans for those with chipolata sausages already incorporated. We often have this as a topping for baked potatoes topped with grated Cheddar! I first learned of frozen trimmed green beans while filming a segment for Jamie Oliver's *Money Saving Meals* TV series. Now, my freezer always has a bag of these ready to throw into various dishes for added nutrition! I love them, as not only are they cheaper than buying fresh green beans, I find that they cook quicker than the fresh ones, perhaps due to the added water content from the freezing/thawing process.

3 tbsp vegetable oil
2 garlic cloves, minced
6 spring onions (scallions), roughly chopped
1 fresh red chilli (serrano), finely chopped
30g (1oz) fresh coriander (cilantro), finely chopped, stems and all
1 tbsp Malaysian Adabi meat curry powder (if you don't have Adabi curry powder, combine ¾ tsp chilli powder, ¾ tsp ground coriander, ¾ tsp ground turmeric, ¼ tsp finely ground black pepper and ¼ tsp ground cumin)
400g (14oz) canned baked beans
400g (14oz) canned oxtail soup (optional, can be replaced with a second can of baked beans)
200g (7oz) fine green beans, fresh or frozen

Heat the vegetable oil in a large non-stick wok or pan over a medium-high heat. Stir-fry the garlic for 10 seconds, then add the spring onions, chilli and coriander, and stir-fry for a further minute.

Add the curry powder, baked beans, oxtail soup and green beans, and bring to the boil, stirring often.

If you're using frozen fine beans, as soon as the whole mixture comes to the boil, turn off the heat and serve. If you're using fresh fine beans, simmer for another 2 minutes before serving.

Add the beans to baked potatoes topped with grated Cheddar. Or, if you prefer, these spiced beans can be eaten simply with rice.

GREEN TURKISH PEPPERS WITH ANCHOVIES

Serves 4

The inspiration for this is from my sister-in-law's father, Low Kim Huat, who pointed out long Chinese green chillies in an East Asian supermarket we visited after a family dim-sum outing. He told me that the green chillies were delicious fried with some *ikan bilis* (dried anchovies) and preserved black beans. I followed his advice and found that, yes, they were indeed delicious with the heat brought by those chillies! My version uses green Turkish peppers, which I can easily find in my local grocers, and substitutes canned anchovies for the *ikan bilis*, and yellow bean sauce for preserved black beans. I also add some bird's eye chillies, as Turkish peppers are generally on the mild side (feel free to leave them out if you wish). I imagine that this recipe would also work really well with Padrón peppers!

1 tbsp vegetable oil
2 garlic cloves, minced
2 bird's eye chillies, finely sliced
  (optional)
25g (1oz) canned anchovies
  (roughly 4 fillets including
  the oil)
1 tbsp yellow bean sauce (or
  ½ tbsp white shiro miso paste)
450g (1lb) green Turkish
  peppers, cut into 2.5cm
  (1in) pieces

Heat the oil in a large non-stick wok over a high heat. Stir-fry the garlic, chillies, anchovies (including the oil from the can) and yellow bean sauce for 1 minute, mashing up the anchovies as you go.

Add the peppers and stir-fry until their skins are blistered. This will take around 4 minutes. Serve immediately.

YELLOW VEGETABLE CURRY

Serves 4

This is a lovely, mild, comforting curry, which would pair well with dry, spicy dishes like the Spicy Coconut Roast Chicken (page 142), Feng Pork Belly (page 159) or the Sambal Skate Wing (page 182). It eats better once cooled and reheated, so I like to cook this curry earlier on in the day to be reheated for dinner, or at the weekend to be eaten during the week.

4 tbsp vegetable oil
1 tsp table salt
300ml (generous 1¼ cups) coconut milk
100ml (scant ½ cup) water
½ tsp white sugar
¼ white cabbage, cut in half, core removed, then cut into 1cm (½in) slices
1 carrot (150g/5½oz), peeled and cut into 5 x 1cm (2 x ½in) batons
200g (7oz) fine green beans, stems removed, cut into 2.5cm (1in) pieces (if using frozen green beans, just throw them in whole!)
small handful of fresh coriander (cilantro) leaves (optional), to garnish

Spice paste
1 tsp ground turmeric
1 tsp chilli powder
1 small onion (150g/5½oz), roughly chopped
4 garlic cloves
1 lemongrass stalk, top, end and any hard outer leaves removed

Using a handheld stick blender, or a high-speed blender like a Nutribullet, blitz the spice paste ingredients to a fine purée.

Heat the oil in a medium non-stick saucepan over a medium heat. Stir-fry the spice paste along with the salt for 5 minutes.

Add the coconut milk, water and sugar, and bring to the boil, then add the cabbage, carrot and green beans. Bring back to the boil, then simmer over a medium-low heat for 10 minutes, stirring every few minutes.

Garnish with coriander (if using) just before serving.

SAMBAL TENDERSTEM BROCCOLI

Serves 4

Chilli and broccoli are a match made in heaven, and turmeric adds a lovely earthy roundness. This gorgeous side dish makes a regular appearance in my meal-planning rotation, as I can swap out the Tenderstem broccoli for a variety of other robust vegetables, e.g. regular broccoli, carrots, cabbage or green beans. And, of course, having my Sambal Tumis in the fridge ready-to-go means I can have this on a weekly basis if I want to!

2 tbsp vegetable oil
2 garlic cloves, minced
400g (14oz) Tenderstem broccoli (broccolini), cut into 2.5cm (1in) pieces
½ tsp table salt
½ tsp ground turmeric
50ml (3½ tbsp) water
2 tbsp Sambal Tumis (page 29)

Heat the oil in a large non-stick wok over a medium-high heat. Add the garlic and stir-fry for 10 seconds, then add the broccoli, salt, turmeric and water. Stir, then cover and cook for 2½ minutes, stirring halfway through.

Add the sambal tumis and stir-fry for another minute. Serve immediately.

GINGER SPRING ONION BEANSPROUTS

Serves 2

This is phenomenally easy to put together if you have Ginger Spring Onion Sauce already in your fridge! I love stir-fried beansprouts – you will often find these accompanying Hainanese chicken rice in Malaysia. Make sure not to overcook your beansprouts, as you don't want them to go soggy – you just want to take the edge off their rawness, maintaining as much crunch as possible. If you want to double this recipe, you'll have to cook it in two batches, as you won't be able to achieve a high-enough heat in your wok with more than 300g (10½oz) beansprouts.

2 tbsp Ginger Spring Onion
    Sauce (page 27)
2 garlic cloves, minced
¼ tsp table salt
300g (10½oz) beansprouts
pinch of ground white pepper
½ tsp pure sesame oil
15g (½oz) bunch of fresh
    coriander (cilantro), roughly
    chopped, stems and all

Heat a non-stick wok over a high heat. Stir-fry the ginger spring onion sauce, garlic and salt for 1 minute, then add the beansprouts and stir-fry for 2 minutes.

Turn off the heat. Add the pepper, sesame oil and coriander, and stir to combine. Serve immediately.

OKRA WITH MUSTARD SEEDS

Serves 4

For best results, please use fresh okra here, as you will get a crispy, crunchy texture with zero slime. Don't be afraid of whacking up the heat under your wok, as this will give a beautiful smokiness to the vegetables. If the heat isn't high enough, you'll just end up steaming your vegetables and get slimy okra, which isn't what we're looking for in this dish. Cutting the okra lengthways, as this recipe calls for, will also help to reduce the slime factor.

350g (12oz) fresh okra

3 tbsp vegetable oil

1 small onion (150g/5½oz), quartered and thinly sliced

1 tsp brown mustard seeds

2 garlic cloves, minced

2 tsp Malaysian Adabi meat curry powder (if you don't have Adabi curry powder, combine ½ tsp chilli powder, ½ tsp ground coriander, ½ tsp ground turmeric, ¼ tsp finely ground black pepper and ¼ tsp ground cumin)

¾ tsp table salt

15g (½oz) bunch of fresh coriander (cilantro), roughly chopped, stems and all

Prepare the okra, leaving the tops on so that the okra is held together while you are cutting through it (rather as you might finely dice an onion). Hold the top of the okra and slice it lengthways from just under the top all the way down to the tip. If the okra is large enough, rotate it slightly (not quite a quarter turn), then slice through again. Only now do you cut the tops off to release the slices.

Heat the oil in a large non-stick wok over a high heat. Stir-fry the onion until the edges turn translucent, around 2 minutes, then add the mustard seeds, garlic and curry powder. Stir-fry for 10 seconds, then add the okra and salt, and stir-fry for 4 minutes.

Turn off the heat and stir through the chopped coriander. Serve immediately.

AUBERGINES IN SPICY YELLOW BEAN SAUCE

Serves 4

Aubergines (eggplants) are, in my view, a seriously underrated vegetable. They are a top-tier flavour sponge and cook very quickly. I like to pair this side dish with a protein main that isn't spicy and isn't stir-fried; e.g. the Lime, Coriander and Shrimp Paste Chicken (page 139) or the Trout with Tamarind, Chinese Mushrooms and Celery (page 199). This way, I can cook the aubergines while the other dish is cooking in the oven or steamer.

3 aubergines (eggplants),
    approximately 600–650g
    (1lb 5oz–1lb 7oz)
6 tbsp vegetable oil
1cm (½in) piece of ginger,
    sliced into thin batons
6 garlic cloves, minced
¼ tsp table salt
3 spring onions (scallions), finely
    sliced, reserve ⅓ to garnish
1 fresh red chilli, finely sliced

Seasoning
4 tbsp yellow bean sauce or
    2 tbsp white shiro miso paste
2 tbsp Tomato Sambal (page 28),
    Maggi garlic chilli sauce,
    Sriracha or chilli sauce of
    your choice
2 pinches of ground white pepper
2 tbsp water

Cut off both ends of the aubergines and discard. Slice in half lengthways and then cut into 3 x 1cm (1¼ x ½in) batons.

Mix the seasoning ingredients together in a small bowl.

Heat the oil in a non-stick wok over a medium-high heat. Stir-fry the ginger for 30 seconds, then add the garlic and stir-fry for a further 10 seconds. Add the salt and the aubergine batons, and stir-fry for 6 minutes.

Add the seasoning mixture, spring onions and red chilli, and stir-fry for 1 minute.

Garnish with reserved spring onions and serve immediately.

CHARRED CHINESE LEAVES WITH FISH SAUCE

Serves 4

This is another dish showcasing the power of *wok hei* (breath of the wok) to transform vegetables into utter deliciousness! If you don't have or don't want to use fish sauce, this dish also works with humble table salt – just add to taste.

3 tbsp vegetable oil
2 garlic cloves, minced
2 bird's eye chillies, finely sliced
3 celery sticks, finely sliced
3 spring onions (scallions),
   finely sliced
1 head of Chinese leaves, cut
   into quarters, core removed,
   then cut into 2cm (¾in) slices
2 tbsp fish sauce
pinch of ground white pepper

Heat the oil in a large non-stick wok over a high heat. Stir-fry the garlic and chillies for 20 seconds, then add the celery and spring onions. Stir-fry for 3 minutes.

Add the Chinese leaves, fish sauce and white pepper. Stir-fry for 3 minutes. Serve immediately.

EGGS

FRIED EGGS WITH BIRD'S EYE CHILLIES AND SOY

Serves 2 as a main meal with rice, or 4 as part of a larger range of dishes

I cannot emphasize enough how much I love eggs – I will have at least two dozen next to my stove at any one time! This dish is a guaranteed hit and comes together in less than 15 minutes from start to finish. It's perfect for whipping up while you're waiting for your rice to cook.

3 tbsp vegetable oil
4 eggs
4 spring onions (scallions), cut
    into 2.5cm (1in) pieces
1 garlic clove, minced
2 bird's eye chillies, finely sliced
1½ tbsp kecap manis sweet
    soy sauce
1 tbsp light soy sauce
1½ tbsp water
fresh coriander (cilantro) leaves
    or more finely sliced spring
    onions (scallions), to garnish

Heat the oil in a large frying pan (skillet) over a medium heat, then fry the eggs to your liking. I like mine crispy on the edges but with a runny yolk. Remove the eggs from the pan to a serving plate, leaving as much oil as possible in the pan.

Increase the heat under the pan to high, add the spring onions and stir-fry for 1 minute, then add the garlic and chillies, and stir-fry for 20 seconds. Turn the heat off and add the two soy sauces and the water. Stir to combine, then pour over the cooked eggs.

Garnish with coriander or spring onions and serve.

OMELETTE WITH FINE BEANS AND OYSTER SAUCE

Serves 2 as a main meal with rice, or 4 as part of a larger range of dishes

Malaysians prefer to have a hot meal for every meal – a cold sandwich just won't do! This is a home-style dish beloved by Malaysians, which you will find on many tables at mealtimes. It's a super-easy, quick and balanced meal that I often turn to for lunch to eat with leftover rice. I would, however, also find it acceptable to have this omelette served hot straight from the frying pan sandwiched between a heavily buttered soft bap.

4 eggs
1 tbsp premium oyster sauce
pinch of ground white pepper
2 tbsp vegetable oil
2 garlic cloves, minced
120g (4¼oz) fine green beans,
    stalks removed and finely
    sliced into rounds

To serve
small handful of coriander
    (cilantro) leaves, roughly
    chopped
chilli oil, to serve

Beat the eggs with the oyster sauce and white pepper in a measuring jug (cup). Mix well.

Heat the oil in a large frying pan (skillet) over a medium heat, then stir-fry the garlic and fine beans for 2 minutes.

Slowly pour the egg mixture into the pan, starting from the outside in. Swirl the pan to spread the egg evenly around it. Turn the heat down to medium and leave for around 15 seconds until the bottom starts to set a little. Gently push one edge of the omelette towards the centre and tilt the pan slightly to let the egg liquid on top flow underneath to fill the empty space in the pan. Repeat around the edge of the whole omelette. Continue to cook for 2 minutes.

Reduce the heat to medium-low, cover the pan and cook for a final 2 minutes.

Serve garnished with coriander and a drizzle of chilli oil.

TOMATO EGGS WITH OYSTER SAUCE

Serves 4

This is an extremely comforting Cantonese dish. I like to add a dollop or two of my Tomato Sambal (page 28) to satisfy my typically Malaysian need for chilli. Imagine a saucy tomato-ey omelette – really lovely with a boatload of rice!

6 eggs
3 tbsp vegetable oil
1 small onion (150g/5½oz),
    quartered and thinly sliced
4 garlic cloves, minced
15g (½oz) bunch of coriander
    (cilantro), roughly chopped,
    stems and all (optional)
400–500g (14oz–1lb 2oz) fresh
    tomatoes, roughly chopped
1 spring onion (scallion), finely
    sliced, to garnish

Seasonings
3 tbsp premium oyster sauce
1 tbsp light soy sauce
½ tbsp pure sesame oil
pinch of ground white pepper
1 tbsp Tomato Sambal (page 28)
    or other chilli sauce/oil of
    your choice

Beat the eggs in a bowl.

Heat the oil in a large non-stick wok over a medium-high heat. Stir-fry the onion for 2 minutes, then add the garlic and stir-fry for 10 seconds. Add the coriander and tomatoes, reduce the heat to medium and stir-fry for 5 minutes until the tomatoes have reached a jammy texture.

Add the seasonings and stir through to make a sauce. Transfer from the wok to a clean bowl.

Pour the eggs into the wok and leave undisturbed for 30 seconds to let them set slightly. Gently scramble until the eggs are nearly cooked through. This should take no more than 2½ minutes. Turn the heat off. The eggs should end up somewhere in between a rough omelette and scrambled.

Push the eggs to one side of the wok. Add the tomato sauce back into the other side of the wok. Gently and loosely fold the sauce into the eggs. Do not incorporate the sauce completely, as you want to end up with big chunks of scrambled egg in between the sauce.

Garnish with the finely sliced spring onion and serve.

SAVOURY EGG CUSTARD WITH SOY AND SESAME

Serves 2 as a main meal with rice, or 4 as part of a larger range of dishes

My mother's meal rotation would often include this standard bearer Chinese home-style dish. It is easy to digest, protein-rich and brilliant for young and old alike. The trickiest part of this dish is getting the water-to-egg ratio correct – all you need to remember is that it is 2:1. Combining room-temperature and just-boiled hot water also speeds up the cooking time. So, for example, if your 4 eggs, once beaten, measure 200ml (scant 1 cup), then you'll need 200ml (scant 1 cup) of room-temperature water and 200ml (scant 1 cup) of hot water. Shallot Oil (page 26) goes very well with this dish, but if you don't have it, sesame oil will do.

4 eggs

room-temperature water, as needed (see above and method for quantity)

just-boiled hot water, as needed (see above and method for quantity)

½ tsp table salt

2 tsp light soy sauce

2 tbsp Shallot Oil (page 26) or sesame oil

2 tsp chilli oil (optional)

1 spring onion (scallion), finely sliced

small handful of fresh coriander (cilantro) leaves (optional)

Whisk the eggs in a measuring jug (cup) and note the volume. Add the same volume of room-temperature water to the egg mixture, then add the same volume of just-boiled water. Add the salt and whisk until thoroughly combined.

Carefully pour the egg mixture through a fine-mesh sieve into two shallow bowls, or four ramekins if you prefer making cute individual portions. Cover the bowls/ramekins with clingfilm (plastic wrap) and gently pierce the middle of each one with a knife to create a steam vent.

Place a steamer rack over a large pan and fill the pan with water until it reaches just below the rack. Cover and bring to a rolling boil over a high heat. Reduce the heat to medium and gently place the bowls/ramekins on the rack. Cover and steam for 15 minutes.

Gently nudge the bowls/ramekins to check if the eggs are cooked – the eggs should wobble slightly in the middle but not be completely liquid. If they are still visibly liquid, keep steaming until they have just a slight jiggle in the middle. You're looking for the consistency of panna cotta.

Remove the bowls/ramekins from the steamer. Spoon over the soy sauce, shallot oil, chilli oil (if using) and sprinkle over the spring onion and coriander (if using). Serve immediately.

SAMBAL BAKED EGGS

Serves 4

My husband and I make this often for our weekend breakfasts. It is very easy to pull together, with just a tinge of spice to wake you up! These baked eggs are reminiscent of North African/Middle Eastern *shakshuka*, but with a Malaysian twist with the addition of sambal tumis.

These would go fantastically with store-bought frozen paratha, which are quite commonly found in supermarkets nowadays. Although any bread will do, really!

3 tbsp salted butter or vegetable oil (45g/1½oz)
1 small onion (150g/5½oz), peeled and roughly chopped
400g (14oz) canned chopped tomatoes or fresh tomatoes, roughly chopped
2 tbsp Sambal Tumis (page 29)
⅛ tsp table salt
4 eggs
finely chopped herbs of choice, e.g. spring onions (scallions), coriander (cilantro), parsley, to garnish (optional)

Heat the butter in a non-stick frying pan (skillet) over a medium heat. Stir-fry the onion for 3 minutes.

Add the chopped tomatoes and reduce for 5 minutes over a medium-low heat until the tomatoes have a jammy texture, stirring every now and then.

Add the sambal and salt, and stir through.

Make 4 wells in the sauce and break an egg into each well. Cover with a lid to cook. If you like your yolks runny, leave to cook for 3 minutes until the top of the yolks have turned opaque; if you prefer your yolks more fully cooked, leave to cook for 4 minutes. Remove from the heat immediately and remove the lid.

Finish with herbs of your choice and serve with cooked paratha or heavily buttered toast.

CORNED BEEF EGG HASH

Serves 2 as a main meal with rice or buttered toast, or 4 as part of a larger range of dishes

This dish uses another canned food favourite of mine – corned beef! The charred crispy bits of this hash are glorious, with addictive pops of heat from the bird's eye chillies. I tend to buy large bunches of coriander (cilantro), as they are cheaper than buying small packs, and I always use the stems as I cannot imagine wasting all that flavour.

2 tbsp vegetable oil
½ small onion (75g/2½oz), finely sliced
4 bird's eye chillies, finely sliced
15g (½oz) bunch of fresh coriander (cilantro), roughly chopped, stems and all (optional)
200g (7oz) canned corned beef, roughly chopped
2 eggs
½ tsp pure sesame oil
crack of black pepper

Heat the oil in a non-stick wok over a medium-high heat. Stir-fry the onion, chillies and coriander for 2 minutes.

Add the corned beef and stir-fry for 2 minutes, mashing it with a spatula as you go.

Push the contents to the side of the wok, leaving a small corner empty. Crack the eggs into this empty corner, leave for 15 seconds, then stir to roughly scramble before incorporating into the corned beef mixture.

Add the sesame oil and black pepper, and stir-fry for 1 minute. Serve immediately.

SCRAMBLED EGGS WITH CHAYOTE

Serves 2

My mum used to cook a lovely side dish for us when we were growing up – scrambled eggs with loofah gourd. I've substituted chayote (chow chow) for the loofah gourd, as chayote is increasingly easy to find in the big supermarkets nowadays. The chayote softens yet retains a satisfying crunch in the middle, and happily soaks up the garlicky sauce, mimicking loofah gourd very well. If you can't find chayote, finely sliced courgettes (zucchini) will also work in this recipe – you don't have to peel them; they will be softer than chayote when cooked, but still as delicious.

2 eggs
2 tbsp vegetable oil
2 garlic cloves, minced
1 chayote (chow chow)
    (300g/10½oz), peeled,
    seeds removed, cut into
    slices of approximately
    6cm x 5mm (2½ x ¼in)
⅛ tsp table salt
pinch of ground white pepper

Beat the eggs in a bowl.

Heat 1 tablespoon of the oil in a large non-stick wok over a medium heat. Pour in the egg mixture and leave undisturbed for a few seconds to let it set slightly. Gently scramble until the eggs are nearly cooked through. This should take no more than 30 seconds. Take the pan off the heat.

Break up the scrambled egg into a few big chunks before removing from the pan to a clean bowl.

Increase the heat to medium-high and add the remaining tablespoon of oil. Stir-fry the garlic for 10 seconds, then add the chayote, salt and white pepper. Stir-fry for 2 minutes.

Add the eggs back to the pan and fold the chayote gently into the eggs. Serve immediately.

OMELETTE WITH ONIONS, CHILLIES AND SOY

Serves 2 as a main meal with rice, or 4 as part of a larger range of dishes

Provided that you are like me and never run out of eggs, this is another brilliant dish to throw together when you are either stumped for what to cook or have very little in your fridge or pantry! Super simple and satisfying.

3 tbsp vegetable oil
½ small onion (75g/2½oz), halved and then finely sliced into semicircles
2 red chillies (serrano), finely sliced
4 eggs, beaten
2 tbsp light soy sauce
pinch of ground white pepper
small handful of fresh coriander (cilantro) leaves (optional), finely chopped

Heat the oil in a large frying pan (skillet) over a medium-high heat. Stir-fry the onion and half of the sliced chilli for 2 minutes until the edges of the onions are translucent.

Pour the eggs into the pan and swirl to spread evenly. Drizzle the soy sauce over the egg mixture in a rough circle and add the white pepper. Leave for around 15 seconds until the bottom starts to set a little. Gently push one edge of the omelette towards the centre and tilt the pan slightly to let the egg liquid on top flow underneath to fill the empty space in the pan. Repeat around the edge of the whole omelette. Reduce the heat to medium and continue to cook for 1 minute.

Cover the pan and cook for a final minute, then garnish with the remaining finely sliced chilli and the coriander leaves before serving.

SPICED BAKED EGG CUSTARD WITH FISH

Serves 3–4

This is based on *otak-otak*, Malaysian spiced fishcakes, which are usually wrapped in banana leaves and then grilled over charcoal. I have converted *otak-otak*'s irresistible flavours into a dish of oven-baked eggs and fish pie mix, which is easier to achieve because you don't have to spend time making the fishcake mixture, nor do you have to wrap banana-leaf parcels!

½ tbsp vegetable oil

2 eggs

3 tbsp Thai red curry paste
(I like Mae Ploy)

¼ tsp shrimp paste (or substitute
with 2 tsp fish sauce)

1 tbsp cornflour (cornstarch)

150ml (scant ⅔ cup) coconut milk

2 fresh red chillies (serrano),
finely chopped

400g (14oz) fish pie mix (if your
store-bought fish pie mix isn't
quite 400g/14oz, top it up with
raw deshelled and deveined
king prawns/jumbo shrimp)

2 fresh makrut lime leaves,
stems removed, finely sliced
(optional)

Preheat the oven to 170°C/150°C fan/340°F/gas mark 3.

Pour the vegetable oil onto a folded-up piece of paper towel and use it to oil a smallish ovenproof dish with a capacity of 800ml (3½ cups).

Whisk the eggs with the Thai red curry paste, shrimp paste and cornflour. Add the coconut milk and chillies before whisking again.

Put the fish pie mix into the prepared dish and spread it out evenly, then pour the egg-coconut mixture into the dish. Place on a baking sheet to make it easier to remove from the oven.

Bake for 30 minutes on the middle shelf of the oven, rotating the dish halfway through. Then remove the dish from the oven, cover it with foil and bake for a further 10 minutes.

Leave to stand for 10 minutes for the egg to set, then sprinkle with lime leaves and serve with plenty of rice.

MEAT AND POULTRY

HAINANESE ROAST CHICKEN

Serves 4

In Malaysia, any eatery that serves Hainanese chicken rice will offer a choice of the more traditional poached white chicken, or a 'roast' version. My preference is usually the roast version, because the chicken is juicy and the skin is packed full of flavour. When researching this recipe, I found out that roast Hainanese chicken is actually fried in most cases. I hate deep-frying at home, so my take on it is very simply oven-roasted. It may look burnt after cooking, but it really isn't – it's just the dark soy sauce! You'll just have to start a few hours before you want to eat, or the night before, to marinate the chicken.

2kg (4lb 8oz) skin-on bone in chicken thighs (12 thighs)
Tomato Sambal (page 28) or other chilli sauce/oil of your choice, to serve
Ginger Spring Onion Sauce (page 27), to serve

Seasoning
3 tbsp honey
1½ tsp five-spice powder
¾ tsp ground ginger
1½ tsp table salt
¾ tbsp dark soy sauce
1½ tsp pure sesame oil
1½ tbsp vegetable oil
pinch of white pepper

Dry the chicken thoroughly with paper towels.

Mix the seasoning ingredients together in a small bowl.

Marinate the chicken in the seasoning for at least 4 hours or preferably overnight. Be sure to get the marinade in between the skin and the meat. I like to marinate the chicken in a large-enough container to hold the pieces of chicken skin-side up in one layer, so that I can leave it in the fridge uncovered. This dries out the skin for better crisping up during cooking.

About 1 hour before you want to cook the chicken, take it out of the fridge. Arrange the pieces of chicken, skin-side up, on a wire rack on top of a large roasting tin lined with foil.

Preheat the oven to 230°C/210°C fan/450°F/gas mark 8.

Roast the thighs for 20 minutes, then remove from the oven. Rearrange the pieces on the wire rack to create more space between the thighs – move any paler pieces from the middle to the sides, and move any pieces with more colour on them into the middle. Rotate the roasting tin and roast for another 15 minutes. Take the roasting tin out of the oven and leave to rest for 10 minutes before serving so that the skin crisps up.

Serve with tomato sambal, ginger spring onion sauce or a chilli sauce/oil of your choice.

Pictured on pages 132–133.

SOY AND GARLIC LAMB CHOPS

Serves 4

One of my earliest food memories is eating chargrilled lamb chops from a man who used to pull up in his little van at dusk at the bottom of Happy Mansions flats in Petaling Jaya, a suburb of Kuala Lumpur. The smell when cooking these lamb chops is incredible, and the taste is out of this world! You will have to start the day before you'd like to eat this, as it involves an overnight marinade for best results. These are also perfect for a barbecue!

12 lamb chops (about 1kg/2¼lb)
1 tbsp vegetable oil, for frying

Seasoning
3 garlic cloves, minced
3 tbsp kecap manis sweet
   soy sauce
2 tbsp vegetable oil
½ tsp chilli powder
1 tsp onion powder
½ tsp table salt

Mix the seasoning ingredients together in a small bowl. Spoon the mixture evenly over both sides of the lamb chops. Leave to marinate for at least 4 hours, or even overnight.

Heat a large cast-iron frying pan or skillet over a medium-high heat until hot. Add the tablespoon of oil to the pan before frying the lamb chops. You'll have to fry them in two batches, as the chops must be kept in a single layer.

Fry the lamb chops for 2–3 minutes on each side, depending on how you like your meat cooked. About 2 minutes will give you medium rare. I like to use a meat probe thermometer to check when the inside of a chop has reached the following temperatures, as this will be the best way of knowing when it is cooked to your liking. Remove from the pan at 57°C (135°F) for medium rare, 60°C (150°F) for medium, or 70°C (160°F) for well done.

Rest the lamb chops on a large serving plate for 5 minutes before serving. They will produce a wonderful jus, once rested. Don't waste any! These lamb chops are superb with rice or any sort of potato.

Pictured on pages 136–137.

LIME, CORIANDER AND SHRIMP PASTE CHICKEN

Serves 4

I started cooking Ainsley Harriot's lime, coriander and fish sauce chicken at university and I think I love London's Kiln restaurant's slow-grilled chicken and soy because the flavour profile is quite similar! I've played around with these two dishes and added shrimp paste as a nod towards a classic Malaysian dish – shrimp paste chicken. This is just as wonderful eaten with mashed potato and salad as it is with rice.

1kg (2lb 4oz) skinless and
    boneless chicken thighs
15g (½oz) bunch of fresh
    coriander (cilantro), roughly
    chopped, stems and all
4 bird's eye chillies, finely
    sliced (optional)

Seasoning
3 tbsp honey
½ tsp shrimp paste (or substitute
    with 1–2 tbsp fish sauce,
    to taste)
½ tsp table salt
6 garlic cloves, minced
1 tsp ground coriander
1 tsp finely ground black pepper
juice of 2 limes (60ml/¼ cup)
1 tbsp vegetable oil

Mix the seasoning ingredients in a small bowl.

Marinate the chicken in the seasoning mixture for 1 hour.

Preheat the oven to 200°C/180°C fan/400°F/gas mark 6.

Put the chicken pieces in a large roasting tin lined with foil. Sprinkle the fresh coriander over the top and roast for 20 minutes.

Sprinkle with the sliced chillies, if using, just before serving, or serve them on the side so that you can tailor the level of chilli heat to your liking.

SOY BRAISED CHICKEN

Serves 4

Every East Asian household will have its take on this recipe centred around comforting soy sauce and notes of ginger. I challenge you to find an easier dish to prepare! Including the eggs is highly recommended, as they pair perfectly with the sauce. You'll usually find skinless bone-in chicken thighs in the halal section of large supermarkets, which is a great time-saver if you can't be bothered to remove the skin from whole thighs, and you'll get more bang for your buck when cooking this recipe!

3 tbsp vegetable oil

5cm (2in) piece of ginger, sliced into thin slices

1kg (2lb 4oz) bone-in skinless chicken thighs or drumsticks

400ml (1¾ cups) water

6–8 hard-boiled eggs (boil for 7½ minutes, run under cold water until cool, then peel)

2 tbsp pure sesame oil

2 spring onions (scallions), finely sliced, to garnish

Seasonings

170ml (scant ¾ cup) light soy sauce

35ml (2 tbsp plus 1 tsp) dark soy sauce

1 tsp ground white pepper

80g (2¾oz/scant ½ cup) dark brown sugar

1 star anise

Heat the oil in a large saucepan over a medium heat. Add the ginger and stir-fry for 3 minutes. Once the ginger is fragrant, add the chicken, water and seasonings to the pan. Bring to the boil, then reduce the heat to the lowest possible level and simmer uncovered for 30 minutes.

Add the whole peeled eggs to the pan in the last 5 minutes of cooking time.

Turn off the heat, then add the sesame oil and stir through.

Garnish with the spring onions and serve.

SPICY COCONUT ROAST CHICKEN

Serves 4

This is a wonderful recipe based on Malaysian *ayam panggang* chargrilled chicken with a spicy coconut sauce, but using store-bought red curry paste. You'll just need to start a few hours before to marinate the chicken for best results. If you like, you can also marinate the chicken overnight.

250g (9oz) UHT coconut cream
   (usually found in a can
   or carton)
2 tbsp Thai red curry paste
   (I use Mae Ploy)
2 tbsp dark brown sugar
½ tsp ground coriander
2 bay leaves
2kg (4lb 8oz) skin-on bone-in
   chicken thighs (12 thighs)
2 tbsp just-boiled hot water
small handful of fresh coriander
   (cilantro), leaves picked

In a medium saucepan, combine the coconut cream, curry paste, sugar, ground coriander and bay leaves. Bring to the boil, then simmer over a low heat for 10 minutes, stirring frequently to dissolve the curry paste and sugar. Remove the bay leaves and allow the sauce to cool.

Use half of the cooled sauce to marinate the chicken for at least 2 hours. Reserve the rest of the sauce.

I like to marinate the chicken in a large-enough container to hold the pieces of chicken skin-side up in one layer, so that I can leave it in the fridge uncovered to air while it's marinating. This dries out the skin as much as possible for better crisping up during cooking.

About 1 hour before you want to cook the chicken, take it out of the fridge so that it comes to room temperature.

Preheat the oven to 230°C/210°C fan/450°F/gas mark 8.

Arrange the pieces of chicken, skin-side up, on a wire rack on top of a large roasting tin lined with foil. Baste the skin with some of the reserved sauce and roast for 35 minutes.

Remove the chicken from the oven. Transfer any thighs whose skin looks brown and crispy to a serving plate. Rearrange the remaining pieces on the wire rack to create more space between the thighs. Rotate the roasting tin and roast for another 10 minutes. Transfer the chicken to the serving plate and remove the wire rack from the roasting tin.

Dilute the remaining sauce with the just-boiled water before pouring it into the roasting tin. Put the tin on top of the largest hob (stove burner) and turn the heat to high for 2 minutes. Using a spatula, deglaze the roasting tin to create a sauce. Carefully drain the sauce from the foil back into the tin and dispose of the foil. Pour the sauce and sprinkle the fresh coriander leaves over the chicken and serve.

GOLDEN FRAGRANT CHICKEN

Serves 4

Kam heong golden fragrant sauce is very popular in Malaysia, and is paired with all sorts of seafood – usually wok-fried crabs, clams or even prawns (shrimp). I've found that it is also delicious with chicken. This is a crowd-pleasing dish, as the chillies in the spice paste are tempered by the sugar and yellow bean sauce.

600g (1lb 5oz) skinless and
   boneless chicken thighs,
   cut into bite-size pieces
1 tsp ground turmeric
4 tbsp vegetable oil
2 fresh red chillies, finely sliced,
   to garnish

Spice paste
1cm (½in) piece of ginger, peeled
   and roughly chopped
2 bird's eyes chillies
4 garlic cloves
1 small onion (150g/5½oz),
   roughly chopped

Sauce
1 tbsp yellow bean sauce or
   ½ tbsp white shiro miso paste
1 tbsp premium oyster sauce
½ tsp shrimp paste (or substitute
   with 1 tbsp fish sauce)
1 tbsp dark brown sugar
1 tsp ground black pepper

Using a handheld stick blender, or a high-speed food processor like a Nutribullet, blitz the spice paste ingredients to a fine purée.

Evenly coat the chicken in the ground turmeric.

Heat 2 tablespoons of the oil in a non-stick wok or large frying pan (skillet) over a medium-high heat. Stir-fry the chicken for 5 minutes to cook it through, then transfer it to a clean plate.

Using the same wok, stir-fry the spice paste in the remaining 2 tablespoons of oil for 5 minutes, then add all of the sauce ingredients and stir-fry for 10 seconds.

Add the cooked chicken back to the wok and stir-fry for 2 minutes to achieve a bit of charring on the chicken.

Garnish with the sliced chillies and serve.

SESAME GINGER CHICKEN

Serves 4–6

This is an extremely soothing dish for when you're feeling slightly under the weather. Ginger pairs so well with the sweetness of rice wine, as well as yellow bean sauce adding a strong umami depth of flavour. It also comes together very quickly and is great for children, as it has no chillies at all. Any alcohol will have evaporated in the cooking process.

1kg (2lb 4oz) skinless and boneless chicken thighs, cut into bite-size pieces
3 tbsp Shaoxing rice wine or Harvey's Bristol Cream sherry
1 tsp table salt, or to taste
2 tbsp vegetable oil
3 garlic cloves, minced
5cm (2in) piece of ginger (50g/1¾oz), peeled and cut into fine 2.5cm (1in) matchsticks
2 tbsp yellow bean sauce or 1 tbsp white shiro miso paste
1 tbsp pure sesame oil
300ml (generous 1¼ cups) water
2 pinches of ground white pepper
2 tsp cornflour (cornstarch) mixed with 1 tbsp water
2 spring onions (scallions), finely sliced, to garnish

Marinate the chicken pieces with the rice wine and salt for at least 1 hour.

Heat the oil in a large non-stick wok or saucepan over a medium heat. Stir-fry the garlic and ginger for 1 minute, then add the yellow bean sauce, sesame oil and chicken, scraping out all the marinade into the wok. Stir-fry for 3 minutes.

Add the water and pepper. Bring to the boil, then reduce the heat to medium-low and simmer for 15 minutes uncovered. Stir every few minutes or so.

Add the cornflour-water mix, stir and cook for 1 minute. Taste the sauce and add more salt if desired.

Garnish with the spring onions before serving with rice.

HANNAH'S LAZY CHILLI CHICKEN

Serves 4

I have my cousin Hannah to thank for this super-easy dish, which I learned from her when we lived together for a while. She too is a busy working mum, and generally will only cook things that involve minimum time and effort. A highly commendable way of thinking! Fresh tomatoes add a lovely acidity to the finished dish – please do not use canned.

2 tbsp vegetable oil
1 medium onion (200g/7oz),
    quartered, then finely sliced
2 garlic cloves, minced
750g (1lb 10oz) skinless and
    boneless chicken thighs,
    cut into bite-size pieces
2 tbsp Sambal Tumis (page 29)
2 tbsp yellow bean sauce or
    1 tbsp white shiro miso paste
2 tbsp chilli oil with bits/chilli
    crisp/chilli crunch
100–120g (3½–4¼oz) fresh
    tomatoes, roughly chopped

To serve
2 spring onions (scallions),
    finely sliced
15g (½oz) bunch of fresh
    coriander (cilantro), roughly
    chopped, stems and all
    (optional)
1 fresh red chilli, finely sliced
    (optional)

Heat the oil in a non-stick wok over a medium-high heat. Stir-fry the onion until the edges turn translucent, around 2 minutes, then add the garlic and stir-fry for 10 seconds.

Add the chicken, sambal tumis, yellow bean sauce and chilli oil. Stir-fry for 10 minutes.

Add the tomatoes and stir-fry for another minute.

Garnish with the spring onions, coriander and fresh chilli (if using). Serve immediately.

MAXINE'S TURMERIC ROAST CHICKEN

Serves 4

This is one of my mum's brilliant recipes, super-simple and quick to throw together. She learned it from one of her Malay colleagues when working in the Malaysian High Commission in London in the 1970s, when they used to have lots of house parties. Parties hosted by Malaysians will always involve plenty of good food! My mum's colleague deep-fried his chicken and only used salt, turmeric and garlic. My mum converted it into an oven-roasted version and added a few tweaks of her own. You'll be surprised at how delicious these are for very minimal effort. If you're gluten free, you can leave out the soy sauce or use a gluten-free version.

1.1–1.3kg (2lb 7oz–3lb) skin-on, bone-in chicken drumsticks (around 11 or 12 pieces)
2 spring onions (scallions), finely sliced, to garnish

Seasoning
1½ tsp table salt
2 tsp ground turmeric
1 tsp garlic powder
1 tsp ground ginger
½ tsp white sugar
1 tbsp cornflour (cornstarch)
½ tsp chilli powder (optional)
1 tsp light soy sauce (optional)
2 tbsp vegetable oil

Mix the seasoning ingredients together in a small bowl.

Marinate the chicken in the seasoning mixture for at least 2 hours. Make sure to really massage the seasonings into the chicken to ensure it fully gets into the meat.

An hour before you want to cook the chicken, take it out of the fridge so that it comes to room temperature. Arrange the pieces of chicken on a wire rack on top of a large roasting tin lined with foil. Make sure there's space between the pieces of chicken for air to circulate.

Preheat the oven to 230°C/210°C fan/450°F/gas mark 8.

Roast for 15 minutes, then remove the chicken from the oven. Turn the drumsticks over. Rotate the roasting tin and roast for another 15 minutes. Take the roasting tin out of the oven and leave the chicken to rest for 10 minutes before serving so that the skin crisps up.

Garnish with the spring onions and serve.

PORK RIB AND DAIKON SOUP

Serves 4

I know this sounds like a bit of a faff, but I now only buy whole racks of ribs so that I can remove the membrane. Ribs that are sold already cut into individual ribs generally still have the membrane on the bony side, which affects the eating experience as it holds all the meat together even when cooked. When I make this soup, I want the lovely tender meat to simply fall off the bones – removing the membrane allows this to happen.

To eat this soup, I serve it with plenty of rice, taking the solids out of the soup onto my rice plate before spooning over a drop of soy sauce and/or some chillies. The soup also acts like a palate cleanser in between richer dishes and reminds me of the *lai tong* complementary soup that you used to get at the beginning of a meal in Chinatown restaurants twenty years ago.

1 rack of baby back pork ribs
 (600g/1lb 5oz)
2 litres (8¾ cups) water
2.5cm (1in) piece of ginger,
 cut into thin slices
5 spring onions (scallions),
 cut into 2.5cm (1in) pieces
600g (1lb 5oz) daikon (mooli)
 radish, peeled and cut into
 2.5cm (1in) chunks
2 tsp salt
2 tbsp goji berries (optional)

To serve
3 fresh red chillies, finely sliced
light soy sauce

Remove the tough translucent membrane on the concave surface of the ribs. Use a spoon to detach the membrane at the thin end of the ribs. Once you get a hold on the membrane, you should be able to easily peel it all the way off. Then slice the rack into individual ribs.

Place the ribs and water into a large saucepan and bring to the boil. Reduce to a low simmer for a couple of minutes or so while you skim off as much of the impurities that rise to the top of the water as you can.

Add the ginger, spring onions, daikon and salt. Bring to the boil again, then simmer over the lowest possible heat, uncovered, for 1½ hours.

In the last 5 minutes of cooking, add the goji berries.

Serve with sliced chillies in soy sauce on the side.

BRAISED PORK BELLY WITH GINGER, VINEGAR AND SOY

Serves 4–6

The inspiration for this dish is a Chinese post-partum confinement dish traditionally made with two types of black vinegar, sweet and normal. I've adapted it to use more widely available ingredients and am pleased to report that it tastes wonderful! The original dish also uses pigs' trotters or pork knuckles for added collagen. Pork belly works just as well here, and the fat just melts away like butter when you eat it. Ginger is traditionally believed by the Chinese to be good for women post-partum, to promote healing and recovery, so is a predominant flavour here.

1kg (2lb 4oz) pork belly slices, skin removed and cut into 5cm (2in) pieces
600ml (generous 2½ cups) water
110ml (scant ½ cup) rice vinegar
50ml (3 tbsp plus 1 tsp) dark soy sauce
100ml (scant ½ cup) kecap manis sweet soy sauce
100g (3½oz/½ cup) dark brown sugar
250g (9oz) ginger, washed and cut into thin slices
2 spring onions (scallions), finely sliced

Place the pork belly into a medium saucepan and add the water. Bring to the boil, then reduce to a slow simmer for a couple of minutes or so while you skim off the impurities from the top of the water's surface.

Add the vinegar, soy sauces and sugar. Place the slices of ginger on top of the pork to help keep it submerged during the cooking process. Bring back to the boil, then reduce to a very low simmer on the lowest possible heat on the smallest hob (stove burner), uncovered, so that the liquid is just very gently blipping away for 3 hours.

Sprinkle the spring onions over before serving.

STIR-FRIED MINCED PORK WITH GREEN BEANS

Serves 4

Chinese Malaysians often use *chai poh* preserved radish in our cooking. Once when I was out of *chai poh*, I used some gherkins that I had hanging around in my pantry instead and was overjoyed to find out that they are a neat substitute! The dried shrimp in this dish adds a gorgeous sweet salinity, and you must add the fresh herbs at the end as they help to lift up the dish. This is a perfectly balanced nutritious dish that can be simply served with rice.

salt, for the cooking water
500g (1lb 2oz) minced
  (ground) pork
2 tbsp premium oyster sauce
½ tsp ground white pepper
2 tbsp dried shrimp (12g/½oz)
  soaked in 60ml (¼ cup)
  just-boiled hot water for
  at least 15 minutes
3 bird's eye chillies, or use
  1 fresh red chilli (serrano)
  for less of a kick
1 small onion (150g/5½oz),
  peeled and roughly chopped
1cm (½in) piece of ginger, peeled
  and roughly chopped
2 garlic cloves
400g (14oz) fine green beans,
  ends trimmed, then cut into
  2.5cm (1in) pieces
3 tbsp vegetable oil
80g (2¾oz) gherkins, thoroughly
  drained of their pickling liquid
  and finely chopped
1 tbsp dark soy sauce
½ tsp dark brown sugar
3 spring onions (scallions),
  finely sliced
30g (1oz) fresh coriander
  (cilantro), roughly chopped,
  stems and all

Bring a medium saucepan of heavily salted water (like the sea) to a rolling boil.

Mix the pork mince with the oyster sauce and white pepper. Set aside.

Drain the dried shrimp with one hand, squeezing all the water out, then finely chop in a food processor. Empty out into a non-stick wok. (You can discard the shrimp soaking water, or reserve it to cook something else another day.)

Using the same food processor bowl, finely chop the chillies, onion, ginger and garlic.

Add the green beans to the saucepan of boiling water and cook for 4 minutes. Drain once cooked.

Add the oil to the wok and stir-fry the dried shrimp over a medium-high heat for 1 minute. Add the chilli-onion mix and stir-fry for 5 minutes.

Add the pork mince and stir-fry for 5 minutes.

Add the fine beans, gherkins, soy sauce and sugar, and stir-fry for 1 minute.

Turn off the heat and stir through the spring onions and coriander, then serve.

FENG PORK BELLY

Serves 4

This is inspired by a dish from the Kristang Eurasian Peranakans. My starting point was from Melba Nunis' Feng recipe in *A Kristang Family Cookbook*, but I have tinkered with it to suit my taste and also vastly simplified it. I usually cook this whenever I have leftover roast meat to repurpose, e.g. after a Sunday roast or Christmas! You can use any meat – chicken, pork, lamb or beef. I've used leftover *siew yuk* Cantonese roast pork belly here, which is the perfect starting point, as it comes already sliced into perfect little chunks to soak up all the wonderful sauce. The sauce uses a touch of vinegar, as is common in Kristang cooking, due to the influence of the Portuguese.

3 tbsp vegetable oil
1 tsp table salt
1 tsp white sugar
1 tsp rice vinegar
500g (1lb 2oz) leftover
    Cantonese roast pork belly,
    or any other leftover roasted
    meat, cut into thin slices of
    around 2.5cm x 5mm (1 x ¼in)
small handful of fresh coriander
    (cilantro) leaves, finely chopped

Spice paste
15g (½oz) dried chilli (red
    pepper) flakes, soaked
    in 100ml (scant ½ cup)
    just-boiled hot water for
    at least 30 minutes
½ medium onion (100g/3½oz),
    peeled and roughly chopped
4 garlic cloves
1 tsp ground turmeric
⅛ tsp ground black pepper
1½ tbsp ground coriander
½ tbsp fennel seeds
½ tbsp ground cumin

Using a handheld stick blender, or a high-speed blender like a Nutribullet, blitz the spice paste ingredients, including the chilli soaking water, to a fine purée.

Heat the oil in a medium saucepan over a medium heat. Stir-fry the spice paste, salt and sugar for 5 minutes.

Add the vinegar and leftover meat to the saucepan. Stir to thoroughly combine, then cover for 3 minutes to reheat the meat. Give it one final stir before garnishing with coriander and serving.

NYONYA TAMARIND PORK BELLY

Serves 4

Peranakans are descendants of Chinese tradesmen who migrated to Malaysia in the 1400s and intermarried with the local women. Women usually took care of the cooking in Peranakan households and are known as Nyonyas. The inspiration for this recipe is a gorgeous Peranakan Nyonya dish *babi assam* tamarind pork, that I tried for the first time at Baba Charlie restaurant in Malacca (my dad's birthplace and a Peranakan stronghold). The original version has a very clear brothy sauce – I've reduced it so that the flavours are more pronounced. Popping the pork belly slices into the freezer for a bit firms up the meat, making it much easier to slice into very thin pieces. You need very thin slices so that the fat becomes soft and juicy after only a relatively short cooking time.

600g (1lb 5oz) pork belly slices, skin removed

1 small onion (150g/5½oz), roughly chopped

4 garlic cloves

3 tbsp vegetable oil

1 tsp shrimp paste (or substitute with 1–2 tbsp fish sauce, to taste)

2 tbsp yellow bean sauce or 1 tbsp white shiro miso paste

2 tsp tamarind paste or Worcestershire sauce (I use Lea & Perrins)

1 fresh red chilli (serrano), finely sliced

300ml (generous 1¼ cups) water

15g (½oz) small bunch of fresh coriander (cilantro), roughly chopped, stems and all

4 bird's eye chillies, finely sliced

Put the pork belly into the freezer for 45 minutes. After this time, very thinly slice the pork belly crossways.

Using a handheld stick blender or a high-speed blender like a Nutribullet, blitz the onion and garlic to a fine purée.

Heat the oil in a large saucepan over a medium heat. Sauté the onion-garlic mix for 10 minutes.

Add the pork belly to the pan and stir-fry until browned.

Add the shrimp paste, yellow bean sauce, tamarind paste, red chilli and water. Bring to the boil, then simmer over a very low heat, uncovered, so that the sauce is just slowly blipping away for 1 hour.

Stir through the coriander before serving. You can serve with bird's eye chillies on the side if you want to keep the chilli kick in the main dish to a minimum, or sprinkle them over the whole dish if you like pops of chilli heat already incorporated.

LAMB AND POTATO CURRY

Serves 4

One of the dishes in my dad's cooking repertoire is a Mamak Muslim Indian lamb curry. He will buy a whole leg of lamb and carve the meat from the bone, trimming off excess fat and sinew before cooking. I don't have the time for this, so have converted his recipe into a quicker one using ready-diced lamb shoulder. The resulting curry is still lovely and rich with melt-in-the-mouth meat. My dad's version doesn't use potatoes, but I love potatoes cooked in a curry, as they soak up the wonderful sauce!

1 medium onion (200g/7oz), roughly chopped

2 garlic cloves

75ml (5 tbsp) vegetable oil

1 tbsp table salt

4 tbsp Malaysian Adabi meat curry powder (if you don't have Adabi curry powder, combine 1 tbsp chilli powder, 1 tbsp ground coriander, 1 tbsp ground turmeric, 1 tsp finely ground black pepper and 2 tsp ground cumin)

2 star anise

4 cloves

1 stick of cassia bark or ½ cinnamon stick

2 cardamom pods, lightly bashed with a pestle to crack the skin slightly

400ml (1¾ cups) water

800g (1lb 12oz) diced lamb shoulder (already trimmed of all excess tough sinew and cut into 2.5cm/1in cubes)

100g (3½oz) canned chopped tomatoes or fresh tomatoes, roughly chopped

300g (10½oz) potatoes, cut into approximately 4cm (1½in) chunks

150ml (scant ⅔ cup) coconut milk

Finely chop the onion and garlic using a food processor.

Heat the oil in a large non-stick pan or a casserole dish (Dutch oven) over a medium-high heat. Stir-fry the onion-garlic mixture and salt for 5 minutes.

Reduce the heat to medium, then add the curry powder, star anise, cloves, cassia bark or cinnamon, cardamom and 200ml (scant 1 cup) of the water. Stir-fry for 1 minute.

Add the lamb, tomatoes and the rest of the water. Stir to combine and bring to the boil, then reduce the heat to the lowest possible. Simmer with the lid on for 45 minutes, stirring every 20 minutes or so.

Add the potatoes and coconut milk. Bring back to the boil, then simmer uncovered for 15 minutes. Taste and add more salt if required.

Like all curries, this eats well the next day once the flavours have developed, but you can also eat it immediately.

MALAYSIAN SPICED LAMB 'KEBAB'

Serves 4

I am a sucker for doner kebabs, so was very taken by Shelina Permalloo's air fryer Friday Fakeaway lamb kebab recipe. That was my starting point, but with the flavour injection of Mamak Muslim Indian *sup kambing* goat soup. Please try to use lamb mince with 20% fat content, as this will give you a gorgeous juicy result – fat is your cooking friend! You just need to marinate the lamb a couple of hours before you'd like to cook it.

1kg (2lb 4oz) minced (ground) lamb
15g (½oz) bunch of fresh coriander (cilantro), finely chopped, stems and all

Seasoning
1 tbsp onion powder (optional, don't worry if you can't get it!)
1 tbsp garlic powder
2 tsp ground ginger
2 tsp ground cumin
2 tsp ground coriander
2 tsp ground turmeric
2 tsp finely ground black pepper
1 tsp table salt

To serve
4 pitta breads, toasted
1–2 tbsp chilli sauce, to taste
2 tbsp Greek yoghurt
handful of fresh salad leaves

Mix all of the seasoning ingredients together in a small bowl.

At least 2 hours before you want to cook, marinate the lamb with the seasoning mixture and chopped coriander. Combine thoroughly using gloved hands.

Tear off two large 40cm (16in) long rectangles of kitchen foil and place on the kitchen counter with the long sides of the foil pieces closest to you. Divide the meat into two small logs and place each log around two-thirds of the way down each foil rectangle. Wrap each one up tightly (like you would a burrito): fold both sides of the foil inwards, then fold the edge of the foil closest to you over the top of the meat, pressing tightly against the far side of the meat, before rolling it up to form a cylinder 25cm (10in) long. Leave to rest in the fridge for 2 hours.

Preheat the oven to 220°C/200°C fan/425°F/gas mark 7.

Place the foil-wrapped logs onto a baking sheet lined with baking foil. Make sure that the openings of the foil are facing upwards to keep the juices of the lamb inside during cooking.

Roast in the oven for 30 minutes, then let the parcels rest for 10 minutes. Open the parcels and place the meat onto a large chopping board. Carefully drain off the meat juices from the foil. Slice the logs on the diagonal into thin slices.

I like to serve the slices of lamb packed into warm toasted pitta bread, with whatever chilli sauce I have hanging around, plus a dollop of Greek yoghurt and some salad leaves.

LAMB MINCE CURRY

Serves 4

This is a wonderfully quick and easy, fail-safe curry, because it uses minced (ground) meat as its main component. My mum used to cook this often, which explains my love for it. I like adding aubergine (eggplant) as well as peas to boost the vegetable content, so that it can simply be served with rice as a fully balanced meal. You can also bake this covered in mashed potato for a slightly different take on cottage pie, as seen in Calum Franklin's *The Pie Room*!

2 medium onions (400g/14oz), peeled and roughly chopped

2.5cm (1in) piece of ginger, peeled and roughly chopped

3 garlic cloves

1 fresh red chilli (serrano), roughly chopped

15g (½oz) small bunch of fresh coriander (cilantro), roughly chopped, stems and all, plus extra to serve

75ml (⅓ cup) vegetable oil

1½ tsp table salt

2 tbsp Malaysian Adabi meat curry powder (if you don't have Adabi curry powder, combine 1½ tsp chilli powder, 1½ tsp ground coriander, 1½ tsp ground turmeric, ½ tsp finely ground black pepper and ½ tsp ground cumin)

½ tsp ground cumin

1 small aubergine (eggplant) (200g/7oz), cut into 1cm (½in) cubes

500g (1lb 2oz) minced (ground) lamb

200g (7oz) canned chopped tomatoes or fresh tomatoes, roughly chopped

200g (7oz) frozen peas

juice of ½ lemon, or to taste

Finely chop the onions, ginger, garlic, red chilli and coriander in a food processor.

Heat the oil in a large pan over a medium-high heat. Stir-fry the onion mixture along with the salt for 5 minutes.

Add the curry powder, cumin and aubergine cubes, and stir-fry for 3 minutes.

Add the lamb and tomatoes, and stir-fry for 5 minutes.

Add the peas and stir-fry for a final 2 minutes.

Add a squeeze of lemon juice, to taste, and a few coriander leaves, before serving.

LAMB CURRY WITH CORIANDER AND SPINACH

Serves 4

This is based on my memories of my dad's takeaways from an Indian restaurant in Finsbury Park, North London, when we were growing up. He used to be in charge of weekend meal planning, so this was an easy win for him. While developing the recipe, I realized that it is essentially a *saag* spinach curry, which explains my love for it, as I love anything that resembles a *saag aloo*. I've added cardamom, cloves and tamarind, as these are common components in Malaysian curries, bringing fragrance and warmth.

1 medium onion (200g/7oz), roughly chopped

3 garlic cloves

1cm (½in) piece of ginger, peeled and roughly chopped

2 fresh red or green chillies (serrano), roughly chopped

70g (2½oz) fresh coriander (cilantro), a small handful of leaves picked for garnish, then the rest roughly chopped, stems and all, plus extra to serve

90ml (6 tbsp) vegetable oil

1 tsp table salt

½ tbsp ground turmeric

½ tbsp ground cumin

2 cloves

2 cardamom pods, lightly bashed with a pestle to crack the skin slightly

800g (1lb 12oz) diced lamb shoulder (already trimmed of all excess tough sinew and cut into 2.5cm/1in cubes)

2 tbsp tamarind paste or Worcestershire sauce (I use Lea & Perrins)

300ml (generous 1¼ cups) water

200g (7oz) fresh or frozen baby spinach

Finely chop the onion, garlic, ginger, chillies and chopped coriander in a food processor.

Heat the oil in a large saucepan over a medium-high heat. Stir-fry the onion mixture along with the salt for 7 minutes.

Reduce the heat to medium, then add the turmeric, cumin, cloves and cardamom pods. Stir-fry for 3 minutes.

Add the lamb, tamarind paste and water. Stir to combine and bring to the boil, then reduce to the lowest possible heat and simmer, covered with a lid, for 1 hour, stirring every 15 minutes.

Add the spinach to the sauce and stir to combine. It is ready when all the leaves have wilted. If using frozen spinach, you'll have to cook for a few minutes longer to thaw and reheat the spinach.

Sprinkle with a few coriander leaves and serve.

BLACK BEEF STEW

Serves 4–6

My favourite Malaysian eatery in London is Dapur in Holborn. You must try their *daging masak hitam* black-cooked beef, if you ever see it on their menu. This is my recreation of it. Sweet, with a deep depth of flavour from soy sauce, but with a hefty chilli kick. You can't help but go in for more!

2 medium onions (400g/14oz), roughly chopped

2.5cm (1in) piece of ginger, peeled and roughly chopped

6 garlic cloves

6 bird's eye chillies

100ml (scant ½ cup) vegetable oil

1.4kg (3lb 2oz) beef cheek, shin or chuck (weight after trimming off all excess tough sinew), diced into 2.5cm (1in) cubes

400ml (1¾ cups) water

1 fresh red chilli, finely sliced

Seasonings

120ml (½ cup) kecap manis sweet soy sauce

2 tbsp dark soy sauce

2 tbsp premium oyster sauce

2 tbsp tamarind paste

2 tsp ground coriander

2 tsp ground black pepper

½ tsp five-spice powder

Finely chop the onions, ginger, garlic cloves and chillies in a food processor.

Heat the oil in a large non-stick saucepan over a medium-high heat. Fry the onion mixture for 5 minutes, stirring every now and then.

Add the beef and water to the pan along with all the seasonings. Stir to combine and bring to the boil, then place on the lowest heat possible on the smallest hob (stove burner). Cover and simmer for 1½ hours, stirring every 20 minutes or so.

After this time, simmer uncovered for 30 minutes to reduce the sauce.

Garnish with the sliced chilli and serve with plenty of rice.

BLACK PEPPER BEEF

Serves 4

When stir-frying meat, East Asians tend to use a very simple velveting technique using cornflour (cornstarch). This helps to tenderize the meat. We will also use thin slices of meat and add plenty of vegetables to help make the meat stretch further. I happily use ready-to-go stir-fry strips of beef found in supermarkets nowadays, instead of slicing thin steaks up by hand. But I will never skip the velveting process! Stir-frying in stages also helps to keep the wok ripping hot, which is key to impart as much smoky *wok hei* (breath of the wok) flavour into whatever you're cooking.

600–700g (1lb 5oz–1lb 9oz) rump steak or ready-to-go beef stir-fry strips
3 tbsp vegetable oil
4 spring onions (scallions), cut into 2.5cm (1in) pieces
2 garlic cloves, minced
1 fresh red chilli (serrano), finely sliced (or use 2 bird's eye chillies for more of a kick)
1 green (bell) pepper, deseeded and cut into 1cm (½in) slices
1 tbsp coarsely ground black pepper

Seasoning
1 tbsp cornflour (cornstarch)
1 tbsp fish sauce
2 tbsp premium oyster sauce
1 tbsp light soy sauce
1 tbsp Shaoxing rice wine or Harvey's Bristol Cream sherry (optional)
½ tsp white sugar
2 tsp pure sesame oil

If you're using a whole piece of rump steak, trim off all excess cartilage/sinew. Cut against the grain into slices around 3 x 1cm (1¼ x ½in).

Mix the seasoning ingredients in a small bowl. Coat the meat thoroughly with the mixture and leave to marinate for at least 30 minutes.

Heat the oil in a non-stick wok over a high heat. Add the spring onions, garlic, chilli, green pepper and black pepper. Stir-fry for 2 minutes.

Remove the cooked vegetables from the wok to a serving plate, leaving as much oil in the wok as possible.

Add the beef to the wok and stir-fry for 5 minutes.

Return the vegetables to the wok, stir to combine and serve immediately.

BEEF CURRY WITH DRIED SHRIMP

Serves 4

John Chantarasak has a beautiful beef curry recipe using shrimp paste in his gorgeous book, *Kin Thai*. This gives a unique surf-and-turf flavour to the curry, irresistible to South East Asians. I've used John's idea, but with dried shrimp and red curry paste instead. Beef cheek is my absolute favourite cut of meat, as it becomes incredibly succulent and juicy after cooking. I highly recommend buying it whenever you see it!

2 tbsp dried shrimp rehydrated in 100ml (scant ½ cup) hot water
1 medium onion (200g/7oz), roughly chopped
3 garlic cloves
1cm (½in) piece of ginger, peeled and roughly chopped
4 tbsp vegetable oil
½ tsp table salt
2 tbsp Thai red curry paste (I use Mae Ploy)
800g (1lb 12oz) beef cheek, shin or chuck (weight after trimming off all excess tough sinew), diced into 2.5cm (1in) cubes
400ml (1¾ cups) water
300g (10½oz) potatoes, peeled and cut into 2.5cm (1in) chunks
225g (8oz) canned bamboo shoots (120g/4½oz drained weight)
1 fresh red chilli, finely sliced, to garnish

Drain the rehydrated shrimp with one hand, squeezing to get rid of as much water as possible. Keep the soaking liquid.

Finely chop the onion, garlic cloves, ginger and shrimp in a food processor.

Heat the oil in a large saucepan or casserole dish (Dutch oven) over a medium-high heat. Stir-fry the onion-shrimp mixture along with the salt for 5 minutes.

Add the curry paste, beef, shrimp soaking liquid and water. Stir to combine and bring to the boil, then immediately move to the lowest heat possible on the smallest hob (stove burner) and simmer, covered with a lid, for 1½ hours, stirring every 20 minutes or so.

After this time, add the potatoes and bamboo shoots and cook, uncovered, for 15 minutes.

Garnish with the sliced chilli and serve with plenty of rice.

HAINANESE BEEF STEW

Serves 4

This dish originated from Hainanese chefs in Malaysia cooking beef stew for their British colonial bosses or customers. The flavour profile is very similar to traditional British beef stew, but typically uses oxtail with the addition of soy sauce and star anise. I've followed this idea but use cuts that are slightly easier to find. I also like adding beans for added cost-effective protein.

1 medium onion (200g/7oz), roughly chopped

3 garlic cloves

4 bird's eye chillies

500g (1lb 2oz) beef cheek, shin or chuck (weight after trimming off all excess tough sinew), diced into 2.5cm (1in) cubes

2 tbsp plain (all-purpose) flour

½ tsp table salt

1 beef stock (bouillon) cube

700ml (3 cups) just-boiled hot water

1 tbsp tomato purée (paste)

1 tbsp light soy sauce

1 tbsp Worcestershire sauce (I use Lea & Perrins)

60ml (¼ cup) vegetable oil

1 carrot, peeled and chopped into 2cm (¾in) rounds

2 celery sticks, chopped into 2cm (¾in) pieces

1 star anise

400g (14oz) canned red kidney beans, drained

Finely chop the onion, garlic cloves and chillies in a small food processor.

Coat the beef in the flour and salt.

Make up the beef stock cube with the hot water in a measuring jug (cup). Add the tomato purée, soy sauce and Worcestershire sauce, and stir well to ensure everything dissolves.

Heat the oil in a casserole dish (Dutch oven) or large saucepan over a medium-high heat. Brown the seasoned beef, then transfer to a clean plate using a slotted spoon, leaving as much oil behind as possible.

Stir-fry the onion mix in the remaining oil for 5 minutes, then return the beef to the pot. Add the carrot, celery, star anise and beef stock mixture. Stir to combine and bring to the boil, then immediately move to the lowest possible heat and simmer with the lid on for 1½ hours, stirring every 20 minutes or so.

After this time, add the kidney beans and simmer uncovered for a further 30 minutes.

Serve with rice or any kind of potatoes.

FISH AND SEAFOOD

SAMBAL SKATE WING

Serves 4

Malaysians love seafood, especially *ikan bakar*, fish grilled on banana leaves over charcoal and slathered in a mouth-watering sambal. Sustainable local skate wings are really great value and have a wonderful delicate, velvety texture once cooked. If you can find skate wings, you'll be rewarded with incredible crispy bits around the edges of the fish to nibble on!

You could also simply use skin-on fillets of other white fish, such as cod or haddock, with a tablespoon of the sambal spread on the top and bottom before grilling skin-side down for 5 minutes, and then another 5 minutes on the other side.

1 tsp vegetable oil
2 x 600g (5¾oz) skate wings
8 tbsp Sambal Tumis (page 29)
1 lime, for squeezing

Preheat your grill (broiler) to the highest setting.

Line a large roasting tin with foil. Pour the oil into the tin and use a folded piece of paper towel to grease the foil.

Place the skate wings fleshiest-side down on the roasting tin. Slather 2 tablespoons of sambal tumis on top of each of the skate wings.

Grill (broil) the skate wings for 8 minutes.

Remove from the grill and turn the skate wings over so the fleshiest sides are now facing upwards. Slather another 2 tablespoons of sambal tumis on top of each wing, then grill for a further 10 minutes.

Serve immediately with a squeeze of lime.

Pictured on pages 180–181.

GREG'S SPICY FRIED PRAWNS

Serves 4

This is an excellent recipe from my dad's repertoire. It is based on a dish he used to have as a child in a Chinese restaurant in Malacca. We know it as *har lok* fried prawns. Yes, this is probably one of the fiddliest recipes in this book, because it requires you to devein prawns (shrimp) while they are still in their shells, but honestly this is really the only preparation you need to do. You can use defrosted frozen whole raw jumbo prawns found in the supermarket freezer aisle for this dish, as they are generally cheaper than fresh chilled ones. The magic of the prawn-infused sauce comes from the tomalley released from the prawn heads and the frying prawn shells. If I had to choose one standout recipe from this book for its stunning flavour, it would be this one. Do try it!

1kg (2lb 4oz) shell-on whole
   prawns (jumbo shrimp)
4 tbsp vegetable oil
2 fresh red chillies, finely sliced
4 spring onions (scallions),
   finely sliced
3 tbsp light soy sauce
110g (3¾oz) ketchup
   (I use Heinz)
¼ tsp chilli powder

Devein the prawns by sticking a toothpick through the second shell joint from its tail and pulling up through the flesh. The vein will become loose, so all you have to do is to pull out the rest of it from the prawn. Use a pair of scissors to trim off each prawn's two long feelers and also snip off the very sharp end of the prawn's head.

Heat the oil in a large non-stick wok over a high heat. Add the chillies and half of the spring onions and stir-fry for 1 minute. Add the prawns and stir-fry for 5 minutes or so until nearly all of the shells have turned red. You can leave the wok for 20 seconds at a time before stirring, to allow the prawns to cook.

Add the soy sauce, ketchup and chilli powder to the wok and stir-fry for a further 2 minutes or until the sauce thickens.

Garnish with the remaining spring onions and eat immediately.

Pictured on pages 184–185.

COD WITH FISH SAUCE, CHILLIES, GINGER AND BASIL

Serves 4

This light, steamed fish with full-on flavour is based on a dish that I saw my friend Izzy Ariff cook in one of her live cook-a-long sessions during the first COVID lockdown. Izzy is from Perak, a northern Malaysian state, close to the Thai border. I expect that traditionally this dish would use Thai basil, but I've found that regular basil is just as lovely. Be sure to spoon plenty of the sauce and herbs onto your portion of fish once it's on your plate!

1 tsp vegetable oil

4 x 120g (4¼oz) fillets of sustainably sourced cod (or other white fish, such as haddock, hake or pollock)

1cm (½in) piece of ginger, peeled and cut into fine matchsticks

1–2 fresh red chillies, finely sliced

1 spring onion (scallion), finely sliced

2 tbsp fish sauce

2 tbsp Shaoxing rice wine or Harvey's Bristol Cream sherry

30g (1oz) bunch of fresh basil, leaves picked

To steam the fish, fill a wok that has a lid with a depth of 4cm (1½in) water and place a trivet inside. If you don't have a large enough wok or a trivet, you can just use a wide deep saucepan with a tight-fitting lid, and a small, upturned heatproof bowl. The lid must be able to close flush once the plate containing your fish is placed on the trivet, and your pan needs to be wide enough for steam to be able to pass around the plate once the lid is closed. Bring the water to the boil. The water must be at a rolling boil before you put your fish in.

Pour the oil onto the heatproof plate you are using for steaming and use a folded piece of paper towel to grease the plate.

Place the fish fillets (skin-side down, if they have skin) on the plate – make sure that there is a little space in between each fillet. Sprinkle the ginger, chillies and spring onion over the fish, then pour over the fish sauce and rice wine or sherry.

Place the plate in your steamer and steam the fish for 10 minutes over a medium heat.

Carefully remove the plate from the steamer and sprinkle the basil leaves on top of the fish. Serve immediately.

SALMON WITH GINGER, HONEY AND CHILLI

Serves 4

My mum used to make this for us. Now that I'm also a mum, I know why – it comes together so quickly with ingredients always found in an Asian pantry, and the little bits of crispy ginger make it irresistible. This sauce goes especially well with oily fish, such as salmon, trout or mackerel, all highly nutritious being full of Omega-3 fatty acids.

4 x 120g (4¼oz) fillets of skin-on wild salmon or chalk stream trout
1 tbsp vegetable oil
5cm (2in) piece of ginger (approximately 50g/1¾oz), peeled and cut into fine matchsticks
2–4 bird's eye chillies (depending on how much you like your chillies), finely sliced
2 spring onions (scallions), finely sliced

Sauce
1 tbsp cornflour (cornstarch) mixed with 120ml (½ cup) water
4 tbsp light soy sauce
2 tbsp honey

Mix the sauce ingredients together in a measuring jug (cup), making sure to start with the cornflour-water mixture first. Set aside.

Pat the fish fillets completely dry with paper towels.

Heat the oil in a large non-stick frying pan (skillet) over a medium-high heat. Fry the fish, skin-side down, for 3 minutes or a bit longer until the cooked opaque flesh reaches halfway up each fillet.

Carefully turn each fillet over and cook for a further minute on the other side, if you like your fish to be just cooked, or 2 minutes if you prefer your fish fully cooked through.

Remove the fish from the pan, leaving as much oil in the pan as possible. Put the fillets skin-side up on a serving plate with a lip to hold the sauce in later.

Reduce the heat under the pan to medium. Add the ginger and chillies to the pan and stir-fry for 1 minute before adding the sauce mixture. Reduce the heat to low and cook for 20 seconds until the sauce thickens.

Pour the sauce over the cooked fish, then sprinkle the spring onions over. Serve immediately.

TUNA WITH CHILLI AND LIME

Serves 1

This is a super-quick lunch I learned from my cousin Hannah, who in turn was inspired by a common Malaysian dish prepared from canned sardines in tomato sauce. Instead of eating it with rice, she pairs it with buttered toast and slices of cucumber and/or avocado for a light lunch. Very simple and so good!

160g (5¾oz) canned sustainably
    sourced tuna
1 round Asian shallot or ½ banana
    shallot (35g/1¼oz), finely diced
a few stalks of fresh coriander
    (cilantro), finely chopped,
    stems and all
1–3 bird's eye chillies (depending
    on how much you like your
    chillies), finely chopped
juice of ½ lime, or to taste
pinch of ground white pepper
⅛ tsp dark brown sugar,
    or to taste
good pinch of Maldon sea salt,
    to taste

To serve
2 slices of buttered toast
a few slices of cucumber
½ avocado seasoned with a
    pinch of Maldon sea salt

Mash all the ingredients together in a bowl. Taste and add more lime, sugar and/or salt, as desired.

Serve spread on heavily buttered toast with sliced cucumber and avocado.

GREG'S SWEET AND SOUR FISH

Serves 4

This is a satisfying dish from my dad's repertoire. A simple sweet and sour sauce with another Malaysian favourite ingredient, tomato ketchup, at its core. Chinese *zi char* restaurants serving affordable home-style fare will typically serve pieces of lightly battered fish with this sauce. My dad used to just stick frozen batter-coated cod fillets in the oven and pour over the sauce once they were nice and crisp! I really don't like deep-frying at home, so I respect my dad's shortcut and highly recommend it!

4 large frozen batter-coated
   cod fillets
2 tbsp vegetable oil
1 small onion (150g/5½oz),
   peeled, quartered and
   finely sliced
2.5cm (1in) piece of ginger,
   peeled and cut into fine
   matchsticks
4 garlic cloves, minced
½ cucumber, halved lengthways,
   then cut into 1cm (½in)
   semicircles
2 fresh red chillies, finely sliced
350ml (1½ cups) water
2 spring onions (scallions),
   finely sliced, to garnish

Seasoning
1½ tbsp cornflour (cornstarch)
   mixed with 3 tbsp water
120g (4½oz) ketchup
   (I use Heinz)
1 tbsp white sugar
2 tbsp rice vinegar
1 tsp table salt
¼ tsp ground white pepper

Preheat your oven before cooking the cod fillets in accordance with the packet instructions. Place them in the oven and add on an extra 10 minutes to the cooking time, to ensure that they are extra crispy.

Mix the seasoning ingredients together in a bowl, starting with the cornflour-water mixture.

Heat the oil in a medium non-stick saucepan over a medium-high heat. Stir-fry the onion and ginger for 2 minutes, then add the garlic and stir-fry for 20 seconds.

Add the cucumber, chillies, water and seasoning mixture. Bring to the boil, then immediately take off the heat.

Pour the sauce into a bowl and garnish with the spring onions.

Serve the fish on a large serving plate. To make sure that the fish stays as crispy as possible, only spoon the sauce over your portion of fish once it is on your plate, right before you are going to tuck in.

HADDOCK WITH YELLOW BEAN AND CHILLI OIL

Serves 4

I used Nobu's famous black cod as a starting point for this dish, but have used yellow bean sauce and added a little chilli kick for a Malaysian twist. This sauce pairs beautifully with white fish.

1 tsp vegetable oil

4 x 120g (4¼oz) fillets of sustainably sourced haddock (or other white fish, such as cod, hake or pollock)

1 spring onion (scallion), finely sliced (optional)

a few stalks of coriander (cilantro), roughly chopped, stems and all (optional)

Seasoning

½ tbsp vegetable oil

3 tbsp yellow bean sauce, or 1½ tbsp white shiro miso paste

1 tbsp honey

1 tbsp Shaoxing rice wine or Harvey's Bristol Cream sherry

1 tbsp chilli oil with bits/chilli crisp/chilli crunch

Preheat the grill (broiler) to the highest setting.

Line a large roasting tin with foil. Pour the oil into the tin and use a folded piece of paper towel to grease the foil.

Place the fish fillets skin-side down in the roasting tin, making sure they aren't touching each other.

Mix the seasoning ingredients together in a small bowl. Use half of the seasoning mixture to slather over the pieces of fish.

Grill (broil) the fish for 5 minutes.

Remove from the grill, turn the fillets over so they are skin-side up and slather over the remaining seasoning mixture. Grill for another 5 minutes.

Sprinkle the spring onion and coriander over the fish and serve immediately.

HOT SOUR TAMARIND FISH CURRY

Serves 4

This is based on a Peranakan Nyonya *assam pedas* hot sour fish curry, full of a Nyonya's favourite ingredients: tamarind, chillies, shrimp paste and lemongrass! It comes together very quickly and has a thin yet punchy sauce.

4 tbsp vegetable oil
¾ tsp table salt
¼ tsp white sugar
3 tbsp tamarind paste or
  Worcestershire sauce
  (I use Lea & Perrins)
1 lemongrass stalk, bruised
  with a pestle
250ml (generous 1 cup) water
600g (1lb 5oz) oily fish (such as
  mackerel, sardines, pilchard,
  salmon or trout – it's fine to
  use fillets), cut into 2.5cm
  (1in) roughly square chunks
200g (7oz) okra, tops sliced
  off, cut into 2cm (¾in) pieces
  either on the diagonal or
  in rounds
½–1 lime, for squeezing

Spice paste
½ small onion (75g/2½oz),
  roughly chopped
2.5cm (1in) piece of ginger,
  peeled and roughly chopped
3 garlic cloves
4 fresh red chillies (serrano),
  roughly chopped
100g (3½oz) canned chopped
  tomatoes or fresh tomatoes,
  roughly chopped
½ tsp ground turmeric
½ tsp shrimp paste (or substitute
  with 1–2 tbsp fish sauce,
  to taste)

Using a handheld stick blender, or a high-speed food processor like a Nutribullet, blitz the spice paste to a fine purée.

Heat the vegetable oil in a medium non-stick saucepan over a medium-low heat. Fry off the spice paste for 10 minutes.

Add the salt, sugar, tamarind, lemongrass and water to the pan, and bring to the boil.

Add the fish pieces and okra, bring back to the boil, then simmer, covered, on the lowest heat for 5 minutes. Do not stir, as the pieces of fish are very delicate once cooked and fall apart easily. Be very gentle when decanting the curry into your serving bowl.

Squeeze over the lime juice to taste before serving.

TROUT WITH TAMARIND, CHINESE MUSHROOMS AND CELERY

Serves 4

Teochew steamed fish usually uses sour plums and Chinese celery for its delicious salty-sour sauce. My cousin Hannah introduced me to her version, which uses the celery more commonly found in the West. She uses lemon juice for the lip-puckering sourness required for this dish, but I prefer tamarind for its slightly sweeter notes.

4 dried shiitake mushrooms (around 12g/¼oz), soaked in 130ml (½ cup) just-boiled hot water for at least 30 minutes

1½ tbsp tamarind paste or Worcestershire sauce (I use Lea & Perrins)

1 tsp table salt

1 tsp vegetable oil

4 x 120g (4¼oz) fillets of chalk stream trout or wild salmon

2 celery stalks, finely sliced

2 fresh red chillies (serrano), finely sliced

To serve

1 spring onion (scallion), finely sliced (optional)

a few stalks of fresh coriander (cilantro), roughly chopped, stems and all (optional)

To steam the fish, fill a wok that has a lid with a depth of 4cm (1½in) water and place a trivet inside. If you don't have a large enough wok or a trivet, you can just use a wide deep saucepan with a tight-fitting lid, and a small, upturned heatproof bowl. The lid must be able to close flush once the plate containing your fish is placed on the trivet, and your pan needs to be wide enough for steam to be able to pass around the plate once the lid is closed. Bring the water to the boil. The water must be at a rolling boil before you put your fish in.

Drain the mushrooms, reserving the soaking liquid for later. Cut off and discard the stalks, then finely slice the caps.

Pour the mushroom water into a small measuring jug (cup) or clean bowl (leave the dregs as you don't want the sediment). Mix in the tamarind paste and salt.

Pour the oil onto the heatproof plate you are using for steaming and use a folded piece of paper towel to grease the plate.

Place the fish fillets (skin-side down, if they have skin) on the plate – make sure that there is a little space in between each fillet. Pour the tamarind-mushroom water over the fish before sprinkling over the mushrooms, celery and chillies.

Place the plate in your steamer and steam the fish for 10 minutes over a medium heat.

Carefully remove the plate from the steamer. Garnish with the spring onion and coriander, and serve immediately.

SPICY TOMATO PRAWNS

Serves 4

This is a super-satisfying dish, which comes together extremely quickly, like all the best Malaysian home-style dishes. It is perfect for when you need a chilli kick and have frozen raw deshelled and deveined prawns (shrimp) ready-to-go in your freezer!

5 fresh red chillies (serrano),
    roughly chopped
2 garlic cloves
5 tbsp vegetable oil
1 medium onion (200g/7oz),
    halved and finely sliced
1½ tbsp dark brown sugar
1 tsp table salt
1 tbsp tomato purée (paste)
2 tbsp water
500g (1lb 2oz) raw deshelled
    and deveined king prawns
    (jumbo shrimp) (defrosted
    weight) – if they're large, as
    pictured, butterfly the prawns
    so that they cook quicker
1 spring onion (scallion), finely
    sliced, to garnish

Using a handheld stick blender, or a high-speed food processor like a Nutribullet, blitz the chillies, garlic and 1 tablespoon of the oil to a fine paste.

Heat the remaining oil in a large frying pan (skillet) or wok over a high heat. Stir-fry the onion slices with the chilli-garlic paste for 2 minutes until the edges of the onions start to turn translucent.

Add the sugar, salt, tomato purée and water, and stir-fry for a minute to fully incorporate everything together.

Add the prawns to the pan and stir-fry for 2–3 minutes until the prawns are completely pink and cooked through.

Garnish with the spring onion and serve immediately.

PRAWNS WITH SPRING ONIONS, GINGER AND TOMATO

Serves 4

Another brilliantly simple recipe that comes together in a flash, provided that you have some Ginger Spring Onion Sauce already in your fridge and ready-to-go prawns in your freezer. But if you have to make the sauce from scratch, it would only take 15 minutes longer to prepare! I love the flavours of this dish as they remind me a little of two popular celebratory Cantonese crowd-pleasers: lobster noodles and steamed scallops with glass noodles. This dish needs fresh tomatoes, not canned.

1 tbsp vegetable oil
6 spring onions (scallions),
 cut into 2.5cm (1in) lengths
400g (14oz) raw deshelled and
 deveined king prawns (jumbo
 shrimp) – defrosted weight,
 if frozen; if they're large, as
 pictured, butterfly the prawns
 so that they cook quicker
400g (14oz) fresh tomatoes,
 halved, deseeded and diced
 (if using cherry tomatoes, you
 don't need to deseed them,
 just roughly chop)
⅛ tsp table salt
2 tbsp Ginger Spring Onion
 Sauce (page 27)
1–2 fresh red chillies (serrano),
 finely sliced (optional)
15g (½oz) fresh coriander, roughly
 chopped, stems and all

Heat the oil in a non-stick wok over a medium-high heat. Stir-fry the spring onions for 2 minutes, then add the prawns and stir-fry for 3 minutes.

Use a slotted spoon to remove the cooked prawns and spring onions from the wok, putting them onto a serving plate. Leave as much of the prawn cooking liquid in the wok as possible.

Add the tomatoes, salt, ginger spring onion sauce, chillies and coriander to the wok and stir-fry over a medium-high heat for 2 minutes.

Pour the prawns, spring onions and any resting liquid from the plate back into the wok and stir to combine, then serve immediately.

TOM YUM MUSSELS

Serves 2

Due to Malaysia's proximity to Thailand, we are generally very fond of fiery tom yum. I personally find chemically produced MSG makes me very thirsty. Since I haven't yet found a tom yum paste that doesn't include MSG as an ingredient, I prefer to use red curry paste instead and add lots of fresh aromatics. Mussels are a relatively cheap seafood, and I can never resist *moules frites*. Already-cleaned mussels are readily available at supermarkets nowadays, so I always pick up a bag if I spy them in the fishmonger section. This is my idea of heaven for a light weekend lunch!

1kg (2lb 4oz) mussels, cleaned
1 tbsp Thai red curry paste
   (I use Mae Ploy)
1 lemongrass stalk, cut in half
   and bruised with a pestle
2.5cm (1in) piece of ginger,
   cut into long slices
3 fresh makrut lime leaves
2 tbsp fish sauce
1 tsp dark brown sugar
200ml (scant 1 cup) water
200g (7oz) Tenderstem broccoli
   (broccolini)
1–2 fresh red chillies, finely sliced
1 lime, for squeezing

At least 2 hours before cooking, soak the mussels in cold water, then rinse and drain once before covering with water again. Leave covered with a clean dish towel in the fridge. Just before cooking, drain the mussels and throw away any with broken shells or that do not close after a gentle tap on their shell.

Add the curry paste, lemongrass, ginger, lime leaves, fish sauce, sugar and water to a large pot with a lid. Bring to the boil, then add the broccoli and bring back to the boil.

Add the mussels, then cover and cook. Give the pot a shake after 3 minutes. If all the shells are open, turn the heat off. If not, continue cooking for another minute or so until all the shells are open (discard any that remain firmly closed). Finish with a scattering of sliced chilli and a squeeze of lime.

Eat immediately, with rice, slices of buttered baguette or with French fries.

INDEX

ACKNOWLEDGEMENTS

Writing a book takes so many people, especially while trying to keep a restaurant afloat and raising a child. All working mums, the hustle is real and I salute you!

Thank you to:

Owen and my family for emotional and childcare support.

My cousin, Hannah Pok, and my parents for so much inspiration for the recipes in this book.

My staff who look after the restaurant day-in and day-out, which allows me to pursue other work and projects (like writing!) that bring me joy. Special thanks to Yao Song Ng – you have been with me for the majority of the last decade, as a customer at my street food stalls and pop ups, as a much-needed pair of hands when the restaurant first opened and now as my phenomenal general manager. The restaurant wouldn't be here today without your passion, care and love.

© Owen Bain

Everyone at Quadrille Publishing – Sarah Lavelle, Sophie Allen, Stacey Cleworth, Katherine Case, Ruth Tewkesbury. Thank you for believing in me and making my vision for this book come true. I have been told by my family that I am quite exacting in my nature, so thank you very much for taking all of my thoughts in your stride. Thanks also to Emily Preece-Morrison for tidying up my copy in quick time.

My photography team – Nicole Herft, Simone Shagam, Louise Hagger, Sophie Levi-Bronze, Alexander Breeze. You are the very best and what we create together is pure magic. Thank you. Shout out to Aldo and Elisabeth Ciarrocchi – I couldn't have asked for a more wonderful studio to shoot in.

© Mandy Yin

© Krishanti Puwanarajah

© Alice Pople

My agent, Nicola Chang, for always fighting my corner, and to David Evans for looking after me on your maternity leave.

Ayse Certel for helping me look and feel my best when it matters the most.

Everyone at *Saturday Kitchen* – Amanda Ross, James Bedwell, Josie Kidner, Matt Tebbutt, Michaela Bowles, Helen McGinn, Olly Smith – for continuing to have me on and for making every appearance such a joy!

The team at Waitrose Food – Lucy Battersby, Laura Price, Ashleigh Arnott. I adore working on projects with you; thank you for always keeping me in mind.

Jamie Oliver and his team. Thank you Jack Deane for having me at the Cookery School. Thank you Jamie for choosing *Sambal Shiok: The Malaysian Cookbook* as one of the first books to feature in your Cookbook Club – seeing hundreds of people all around the world cooking my recipes was an ethereal experience. Thank you also for featuring me in your Money Saving Meals series. It has been such a blessing opening the restaurant just down the road from your HQ.

My Cheerleaders – Friends and Industry supporters:

• Everyone in my regular whatsapps – Guan Leong Chua, Lap-fai and Connie Lee, Colin Tu, Ping Coombes, Sandra Leong, Ae-Mi Soon, Kar Shing Tong, Chris and Natasha Keeling, Sarah and Justin Ellis, Lucy Hall, Elina Man, Julia Foye, Tashvin Ramdarshan, Thash Pillay, Richard Wong, Krupali Sheth, Gabija Abley, Theresa Hickman, Tom Ma. I very much appreciate your friendship, honesty and humour, through thick and thin. My life is richer with you in it. Special shout out to David Motion, you've supplied my business with delicious wine for nearly a decade and your enthusiasm for what we do at the restaurant is truly wonderful.

© Owen Bain

• Fellow food writers and authors – Meera Sodha, Ching-He Huang, Rachel Khoo, Tom Parker-Bowles, Emily and Amy Chung, Jenny Lau, Melissa Thompson, Ravneet Gill, Anna Sulan Masing, Tom Zahir Browne, Sharon Wee, David Jay Paw, Ed Smith, Georgina Hayden, Tim Anderson and Claire Thomson. Thank you for your advice, for sounding out my worries and for inspiring me to keep going.

• Everyone at Opentable for championing Sambal Shiok Laksa Bar and I. Being on your UK Restaurant Advisory Board has been such an unexpected gift.

Last but not least, all customers of the restaurant and everyone who has bought my books. I wouldn't be able to do what I do without your support. Thank you.

© Angus Raffle

© Mandy Yin

© Owen Bain

ACKNOWLEDGEMENTS

ABOUT THE AUTHOR

Mandy Yin is Malaysian-born Chinese of Peranakan Nyonya heritage. She moved from Kuala Lumpur to London at 11 and later studied and practised corporate law. She eventually gave this up for a career in food. Mandy watched her mother cook all the family dishes they'd eaten for years and meticulously wrote down every step. She combined this knowledge of the fundamentals of Malaysian cuisine – its mind-boggling array of snacks, sharing dishes, slow-cooked curries and stews, strong spices and deep flavours, famous spicy laksa noodle soup and the nation's beloved sambal chilli sauce – with her memories of boisterous, hot hawker centres in Kuala Lumpur.

Her life goal is to showcase Malaysian food and its accessibility. Spicy and/or powerful flavours are Mandy's calling card. She has steadily built a loyal following for her unique dishes, drawing on her food memories of growing up in Kuala Lumpur and dinners at home with her family, mixed in with her London favourites and travel inspirations.

Now, Mandy owns and runs cult restaurant Sambal Shiok Laksa Bar in Highbury, North London, which won Ching He Huang's Best Innovation Award at the Golden Chopsticks Awards, 2019.

In 2024, she worked with Jigsaw as a brand ambassador, was the official ambassador for Battersea Power Station's inaugural CelebrASIA festival and was appointed to OpenTable UK's Restaurant Advisory Board.

Mandy has been featured in Code Hospitality's 100 Most Influential Women (2019, 2021, 2022) and won the Be Inclusive Hospitality Spotlight Chef of the Year Award 2024.

She has appeared on BBC One's *Saturday Kitchen Live* and *MasterChef: The Professionals*, *Newsnight*, *ITV News*, as well as BBC Radio London and BBC Radio 4. She writes for publications such as the *Guardian*, *Observer Food Monthly* and *Waitrose Food*.

The first print of her debut cookbook, *Sambal Shiok: The Malaysian Cookbook*, sold out in less than two months of release in 2021 and was nominated for several food writing awards in 2022.

Sambal Shiok was also chosen as Jamie Oliver's Cookbook Club's book of the month in February 2022, where hundreds of people internationally cooked daily from it.

Since the success of *Sambal Shiok*, Mandy has become a mother to her son, Rhion, which sees her juggling childcare and household responsibilities while keeping her restaurant afloat and tending to other work commitments. Her focus now is simple – fuss-free Malaysian-inspired cooking to feed her family as quickly and as satisfyingly as possible.

Quadrille, Penguin Random House UK, One Embassy Gardens, 8 Viaduct Gardens, London SW11 7BW

Quadrille Publishing Limited is part of the Penguin Random House group of companies whose addresses can be found at global.penguinrandomhouse.com

Penguin
Random House
UK

Published by Quadrille in 2025

www.penguin.co.uk

A CIP catalogue record for this book is available from the British Library

ISBN 978-1-83783-241-5
10 9 8 7 6 5 4 3 2 1

Publishing Director Sarah Lavelle
Editorial Director Sophie Allen
Designer Katherine Case
Project Editor Stacey Cleworth
Photographer Louise Hagger
Photographer's Assistant Sophie Levi-Bronze
Props Stylist Alexander Breeze
Food Stylist Nicole Herft
Food Stylist's Assistant Simone Shagam
Production Director Stephen Lang
Production Manager Sabeena Atchia

Colour reproduction by F1

Printed in China by RR Donnelley APS

The authorised representative in the EEA is Penguin Random House Ireland, Morrison Chambers, 32 Nassau Street, Dublin D02 YH68.

Penguin Random House is committed to a sustainable future for our business, our readers and our planet. This book is made from Forest Stewardship Council® certified paper.